Volume 2

Best RECIPES Ever

TRANSCONTINENTAL BOOKS

5800 Saint-Denis St.
Suite 900
Montreal, Que. H2S 3L5
Tel: 514-273-1066
Toll-free: 1-800-565-5531
canadianliving.com

Bibliothèque et Archives nationales du
Québec and Library and Archives Canada
cataloguing in publication

Main entry under title:
Best recipes ever: fresh, fun & tasty
tested-till-perfect recipes from the hit show
Subtitle of v. 2: more fresh, fun & tasty tested-
till-perfect recipes from the hit show
Includes index.
"Canadian Living, CBC".
ISBN 978-1-927632-00-0 (v. 2)
1. Quick and easy cooking. 2. Low budget
cooking. I. Canadian Broadcasting Corporation.
II. Title : Canadian living.

TX833.5.B47 2011   641.5'55
C2010-942529-4

Project editor: Tina Anson Mine
Copy editor: Brenda Thompson
Indexer: Beth Zabloski
Art direction and design: Chris Bond,
Colin Elliott

Printed in Canada
© Transcontinental Books and
Canadian Broadcasting Corporation, 2013
Legal deposit – 3rd quarter 2013
National Library of Quebec
National Library of Canada
ISBN 978-1-927632-00-0 (v. 2)

We acknowledge the financial support of
our publishing activity by the Government
of Canada through the Canada Book Fund.

For information on special rates for
corporate libraries and wholesale purchases,
please call 1-866-800-2500.

Canadian Living

CBC

Volume 2

Best RECIPES Ever

MORE FRESH, FUN & TASTY
TESTED-TILL-PERFECT RECIPES
FROM THE HIT SHOW

Transcontinental Books

A note from Christine

Being the host of *Best Recipes Ever* – and getting to cook with you every afternoon – is a dream come true.

Ever since I was a little girl growing up in Newfoundland, I have felt at home in the kitchen. (East Coasters know that's where the party always starts!) Whether I was baking bread with my mother or making my first batch of chocolate chip cookies all by myself, I knew that if I could spend my life cooking, I would have the best job in the world.

When I was told I had been chosen to be the host of *Best Recipes Ever* over 450 other hopefuls, I was beyond honoured. I had been a fan of this superpopular CBC show since it started and now I was being given the chance to visit your homes every afternoon and cook my way through *Canadian Living*'s Tested-Till-Perfect recipe library.

So why was *Best Recipes Ever* important to me as a viewer? The recipes from The Canadian Living Test Kitchen speak to me – they are simple, always delicious and made from scratch using ingredients I usually have on hand. And since they're Tested Till Perfect, my money, time and energy are spent making dishes I know will work out – every time.

When you write to us on Facebook and Twitter, I hear that we have the same challenges. Like you, I'm a busy mom with a million things on the go, like shuttling my daughter to hip-hop dance class or my son to basketball games. I understand it's not always easy to put a homemade meal on the table, but *Best Recipes Ever* and this cookbook are here to help.

In these pages, you'll find tasty solutions to real-life mealtime dilemmas. Roasted or braised chicken is one of my go-tos each week, and Chicken With 40 Cloves of Garlic (page 103) will make your kitchen smell just as heavenly as mine does when I cook it. Lemongrass Pork Tenderloin With Stir-Fried Quinoa (page 109) is amazing – it's easy enough for a weeknight dinner but fancy enough for entertaining. And save room for dessert, because Classic Tarte Tatin (page 241), full of apples and caramel, is a foolproof way to finish any dinner with rustic French flair.

And don't miss the "Best Tips Ever" tabs that appear at the bottom of the recipe pages. They're loaded with time-saving tricks, make-ahead ideas and helpful ingredient notes that will make your kitchen prep even easier.

More than anything, I hope we encourage you to get cooking. Pick a dish (any dish!) and give it a whirl. When you make food from scratch, you know what your family is eating and you'll feel good about it. It will also help build your confidence to try more recipes. Get your kids involved too. Maybe they'll be inspired to make their own first-ever batch of chocolate chip cookies.

I hope this cookbook and these delicious *Canadian Living* recipes find a well-loved home in your kitchen.

All the *Best*,

Christine Tizzard, host, *Best Recipes Ever*

Top: Christine Tizzard, host of *Best Recipes Ever*. Bottom (left to right): The Canadian Living Test Kitchen – senior food specialist Rheanna Kish, food specialist Irene Fong, food director Annabelle Waugh, and food specialists Jennifer Bartoli and Amanda Barnier.

contents

weeknight dinners

Chicken Cutlets With Cilantro Peanut Sauce

This green herb-based sauce is like an Asian-style pesto. It's equally nice on your favourite type of mild grilled fish. This sauce is also a time-saver – you can make it ahead and just bring it back up to room temperature before serving.

1½ cups packed **fresh parsley**

½ cup packed **fresh cilantro**

⅓ cup chopped **unsalted roasted peanuts**

¼ cup **peanut oil** or vegetable oil

2½ tbsp **white wine vinegar**

½ tsp each **salt** and **pepper**

4 **boneless skinless chicken breasts**

Finely chop parsley and cilantro; transfer to bowl. Stir in peanuts, all but 2 tsp of the oil, the vinegar and half each of the salt and pepper. Set aside. *(Make-ahead: Cover and refrigerate for up to 2 days.)*

Between plastic wrap, pound chicken with meat mallet or bottom of heavy skillet to ¼-inch (5 mm) thickness. Brush with remaining oil; sprinkle with remaining salt and pepper.

Place chicken on greased grill over medium-high heat; close lid and grill, turning once, until chicken is no longer pink inside, about 5 minutes. To serve, spoon sauce over chicken.

Makes 4 servings. PER SERVING: about 347 cal, 34 g pro, 22 g total fat (4 g sat. fat), 4 g carb, 2 g fibre, 79 mg chol, 422 mg sodium, 597 mg potassium. % RDI: 5% calcium, 16% iron, 21% vit A, 52% vit C, 25% folate.

fast weeknight mains

Zucchini & Ricotta Shells

Creamy ricotta cheese is wonderful with simple flavourings – just a bit of lemon, salt and pepper is all it needs. Serve this pasta with a quick green salad for an appealing, light dinner.

4 cups medium or large **shell pasta**

½ cup **ricotta cheese**

1 tsp grated **lemon zest**

½ tsp **salt**

¼ tsp **pepper**

2 **zucchini**

1 tbsp **extra-virgin olive oil**

2 tbsp thinly sliced **fresh mint**

2 tbsp thinly sliced **green onions**
   (green parts only)

2 tbsp **lemon juice**

In saucepan of boiling salted water, cook pasta according to package instructions until al dente. Reserving ½ cup of the cooking liquid, drain. In large bowl, toss together pasta, ricotta cheese, lemon zest, salt, pepper and half of the reserved cooking liquid.

Meanwhile, quarter each zucchini lengthwise. With knife, cut away core; cut diagonally into slices.

In skillet, heat oil over medium-high heat; sauté zucchini until tender, about 5 minutes. Add to pasta along with mint, green onions, lemon juice and enough of the remaining cooking liquid for desired creaminess; toss to coat.

Makes 4 servings. PER SERVING: about 404 cal, 14 g pro, 9 g total fat (3 g sat. fat), 66 g carb, 5 g fibre, 16 mg chol, 580 mg sodium, 282 mg potassium. % RDI: 9% calcium, 26% iron, 12% vit A, 12% vit C, 84% folate.

Black Forest Ham & Gruyère Frittata

On-hand staples make this frittata a must-have recipe for hectic weeknights.

2 tbsp **butter**

1 cup thinly sliced **leeks**
  (white and light green parts only)

1 clove **garlic,** minced

8 **eggs**

¼ tsp **salt**

Pinch **pepper**

1 cup diced **Black Forest ham**

¾ cup shredded **Gruyère cheese**

¼ cup chopped **fresh parsley**

In 9- or 10-inch (23 or 25 cm) ovenproof nonstick skillet, melt butter over medium heat; cook leeks and garlic, stirring occasionally, until leeks are softened and golden, about 6 minutes.

In bowl, whisk together eggs, ¼ cup water, salt and pepper; pour over leek mixture. Sprinkle with ham, Gruyère cheese and parsley; cook over medium-low heat until bottom and side are firm but top is still runny, about 7 minutes.

Broil until frittata is golden and set, about 2 minutes.

Makes 4 to 6 servings. PER EACH OF 6 SERVINGS: about 222 cal, 17 g pro, 16 g total fat (7 g sat. fat), 3 g carb, trace fibre, 285 mg chol, 513 mg sodium, 210 mg potassium. % RDI: 17% calcium, 9% iron, 19% vit A, 7% vit C, 20% folate.

Steak & Black Bean Stir-Fry

Stir-fries are another great weeknight meal – once the ingredients are prepped, dinner is ready in minutes.

12 oz (340 g) **top sirloin grilling steak**

4 tsp **cornstarch**

1 tsp minced **fresh ginger**

2 tbsp **black bean garlic sauce** (see Tip, below)

1 tsp **hot pepper sauce**

1 tbsp **vegetable oil**

1 **onion,** sliced

2 cloves **garlic,** minced

¾ cup thinly sliced **carrots**

¾ cup thinly sliced **celery**

1 can (8 oz/227 mL) **sliced water chestnuts,** drained

1 cup **snow peas**

Thinly slice beef across the grain; place in bowl. Add 1 tsp of the cornstarch, ginger and 1 tsp water; toss to coat. Stir together ¾ cup water, remaining cornstarch, black bean garlic sauce and hot pepper sauce. Set aside separately.

In wok, heat half of the oil over high heat; stir-fry beef until browned, about 1 minute. Transfer to plate. Add remaining oil to wok; stir-fry onion, garlic, carrots, celery and water chestnuts until tender-crisp, about 2 minutes. Add snow peas; stir-fry for 1 minute. Add beef and sauce mixture; boil until thickened, about 1 minute.

Makes 4 servings. PER SERVING: about 229 cal, 21 g pro, 7 g total fat (2 g sat. fat), 20 g carb, 3 g fibre, 40 mg chol, 224 mg sodium. % RDI: 4% calcium, 22% iron, 52% vit A, 23% vit C, 13% folate.

best **TIPS** ever

Look for black bean garlic sauce at Chinese or Asian grocery stores, or in the Asian condiment section of the supermarket. Different brands vary in saltiness – experiment to find your favourite.

Burrito Stack

This kid-friendly recipe has all the flavours of a burrito in a fun-to-eat format. Black beans make a nice substitute for the red kidney beans if you have them. Short on time? Buy shredded cheese or a cheese blend, such as Tex-Mex.

12 oz (340 g) **lean ground beef**

1 **onion,** chopped

4 cloves **garlic,** minced

4 tsp **chili powder**

½ tsp **dried oregano**

¼ tsp each **salt** and **cayenne pepper**

1 can (19 oz/540 mL) **red kidney beans,** drained and rinsed

¾ cup **salsa**

4 **large flour tortillas**

1 cup shredded **Cheddar cheese** or Monterey Jack cheese

1 cup shredded **lettuce**

½ cup **light sour cream**

In nonstick skillet, cook beef, onion and garlic over medium-high heat, breaking up with spoon, until beef is no longer pink, about 5 minutes. Stir in chili powder, oregano, salt and cayenne pepper; cook for 2 minutes.

In large bowl, mash kidney beans; stir in ¼ cup of the salsa. Add beef mixture; stir to blend.

Place 1 tortilla on rimmed baking sheet; spread one-third of the beef mixture right to edge of tortilla, then sprinkle with one-quarter of the Cheddar cheese. Repeat layers twice. Top with remaining tortilla and cheese.

Bake in 450°F (230°C) oven until cheese is melted, about 10 minutes. Slice into wedges; top with lettuce, sour cream and remaining salsa.

Makes 4 servings. PER SERVING: about 663 cal, 39 g pro, 29 g total fat (13 g sat. fat), 63 g carb, 12 g fibre, 82 mg chol, 1,135 mg sodium. % RDI: 32% calcium, 41% iron, 23% vit A, 25% vit C, 37% folate.

easy mexican dinner

Black Bean Corn Salsa

This chunky salsa is great with tortilla chips, of course, as well as grilled meats. But it also makes a fresh, simple side dish.

2 cobs **corn** (unhusked)

2 **sweet green peppers**

1 cup **cooked black beans**
   (see Tips, below)

⅓ cup chopped **fresh cilantro**

¼ cup finely chopped **red onion**

1 **jalapeño pepper,** seeded and diced

3 tbsp **lime juice**

3 tbsp **vegetable oil**

½ tsp each **salt** and **ground cumin**

Trim loose silk off corn; soak unhusked corn in water for 10 minutes. Place corn and green peppers on grill over medium-high heat; close lid and grill, turning occasionally, until tender and charred, about 10 minutes. Let cool.

Peel husks and silk from corn; cut kernels off cobs. Transfer to large bowl. Peel and chop peppers; add to corn.

Add black beans, cilantro, onion, jalapeño pepper, lime juice, oil, salt and cumin; toss well to combine. *(Make-ahead: Refrigerate in airtight container for up to 24 hours.)*

Makes 6 to 8 servings. PER EACH OF 8 SERVINGS: about 118 cal, 3 g pro, 6 g total fat (1 g sat. fat), 16 g carb, 3 g fibre, 0 mg chol, 151 mg sodium. % RDI: 1% calcium, 6% iron, 2% vit A, 42% vit C, 24% folate.

best
TIPS
ever

• Dried black beans usually need to be soaked overnight before cooking. Instead, you can gently boil beans in three times their volume of water for 2 minutes. Remove from heat, cover and let stand for 1 hour. Drain. Cover beans again with three times their volume of water and bring to boil. Reduce heat, cover and simmer until tender, about 30 minutes.

• To speed up this recipe even more, use 1 cup rinsed drained canned black beans instead of the cooked dried ones. Reduce salt to ¼ tsp.

Chayote Salad These mild, pale green Latin American squashes are now common in the produce section.

3 small **chayotes** (unpeeled)

3 tbsp **extra-virgin olive oil**

2 tbsp **lime juice**

Half small clove **garlic,** grated

¼ tsp each **salt** and **pepper**

2 tbsp chopped **fresh cilantro**

In saucepan of boiling salted water, cook chayotes until tender-crisp, about 5 minutes. Drain and chill under cold water; drain well. Thinly slice; pat dry with paper towels.

In large bowl, whisk together oil, lime juice, garlic, salt and pepper. Add chayotes and cilantro; toss to coat.

Makes 6 servings. PER SERVING: about 80 cal, 1 g pro, 7 g total fat (1 g sat. fat), 4 g carb, 2 g fibre, 0 mg chol, 276 mg sodium, 139 mg potassium. % RDI: 1% calcium, 2% iron, 1% vit A, 12% vit C, 6% folate.

change it up
Zucchini Salad: Instead of the chayotes, use 3 small untrimmed zucchini (1 lb/450 g); simmer, whole, until tender-crisp, about 7 minutes.

Classic Margarita White or gold tequila works just fine here. The better the tequila, the better the cocktail.

1½ cups **tequila**

½ cup **clear orange-flavoured liqueur**
   (such as Cointreau or Triple Sec)

⅓ cup **lime juice**

Ice cubes

GARNISHES:

Coarse salt

Lime wedges

In pitcher, stir together tequila, orange-flavoured liqueur and lime juice. Top with ice; stir well to blend and chill.

GARNISHES: Rim glasses with coarse salt; strain margarita mixture into glasses. Garnish with lime wedges.

Makes 8 servings. PER SERVING (WITHOUT GARNISHES): about 162 cal, 0 g pro, trace total fat (0 g sat. fat), 8 g carb, 0 g fibre, 0 mg chol, 1 mg sodium, 13 mg potassium. % RDI: 5% vit C.

change it up
Strawberry Margarita: Stir in 1 cup puréed frozen strawberries. Garnish each glass with 1 fresh strawberry.

Kiwi Margarita: Stir in 1 cup puréed peeled cored kiwifruits (about 8). Garnish each glass with 1 slice kiwifruit and 1 fresh strawberry.

Jalapeño & Tuna Potato Salad

Excellent served warm or cool, this main-course salad is a jazzy addition to a picnic menu. You can substitute 2 tbsp minced pickled jalapeño peppers for the fresh if it's more convenient. Or turn up the heat by adding an extra jalapeño.

5 **yellow-fleshed potatoes** (about 2 lb/ 900 g total), scrubbed

Half **red onion,** thinly sliced

2 cans (each 6 oz/170 g) **chunk light tuna,** drained and broken in chunks

⅓ cup **extra-virgin olive oil**

¼ cup chopped **fresh parsley**

¼ cup **wine vinegar**

1 **jalapeño pepper,** seeded and minced

1 tbsp **capers,** drained and minced

¼ tsp each **salt** and **pepper**

In large pot of boiling salted water, cover and cook potatoes until tender, about 25 minutes. Drain and let cool. Cut into 1-inch (2.5 cm) cubes.

In large bowl, combine potatoes, onion and tuna. Whisk together oil, parsley, vinegar, jalapeño pepper, capers, salt and pepper; pour over potato mixture and gently toss to coat. *(Make-ahead: Cover and refrigerate for up to 2 days.)*

Makes 4 to 6 servings. PER EACH OF 6 SERVINGS: about 273 cal, 14 g pro, 12 g total fat (2 g sat. fat), 27 g carb, 2 g fibre, 13 mg chol, 547 mg sodium. % RDI: 2% calcium, 10% iron, 4% vit A, 38% vit C, 11% folate.

change it up

Jalapeño & Chicken Potato Salad: Omit tuna; add 2 cooked boneless skinless chicken breasts, cubed.

Jalapeño & Salmon Potato Salad: Omit tuna; add 2 cans (each 6½ oz/184 g) sockeye salmon, drained and broken in chunks.

dinners from the pantry

Moroccan Vegetable Pie With Chickpea Crust

Chickpeas and spices make the crust of this hearty pie fragrant and dense. Though there are a number of ingredients in this recipe, many are pantry staples and the dish makes an impressive entrée.

2 tbsp **vegetable oil**

1 each **onion** and **carrot,** diced

1 clove **garlic,** minced

1 tsp **cinnamon**

½ tsp each **ground coriander**
    and **ground cumin**

½ tsp each **salt** and **pepper**

¼ tsp **cayenne pepper**

1 **sweet yellow pepper** or
    sweet red pepper, diced

1 **zucchini,** diced

3 cups small **cauliflower florets**

1 cup rinsed drained **canned chickpeas**

1 cup **tomato pasta sauce**

1 tbsp **lemon juice**

1 cup **frozen peas**

2 tbsp chopped **fresh cilantro**
    or parsley

2 tbsp **almond butter** or
    peanut butter

CHICKPEA CRUST:

1 cup rinsed drained **canned chickpeas**

⅓ cup cold **butter,** cubed

1 tsp **salt**

½ tsp each **ground cumin**
    and **turmeric**

1½ cups **all-purpose flour**

1 tbsp **milk** or soy milk

In large saucepan, heat oil over medium heat; cook onion, carrot, garlic, cinnamon, coriander, cumin, salt, pepper and cayenne pepper, stirring often, until softened, about 5 minutes.

Add yellow pepper, zucchini, cauliflower and chickpeas; cook, stirring often, until yellow pepper is softened, about 8 minutes.

Stir in pasta sauce and lemon juice; cover and simmer over low heat until vegetables are tender, 20 minutes. Stir in peas, cilantro and almond butter; let cool. *(Make-ahead: Refrigerate in airtight container for up to 24 hours. Let stand at room temperature for 20 minutes before continuing.)*

CHICKPEA CRUST: Meanwhile, in food processor, pulse together chickpeas, butter, 3 tbsp cold water, salt, cumin and turmeric until crumbly. Add flour; pulse until combined.

Turn out onto floured surface; knead until smooth, about 2 minutes. Cut in half; roll out each into 10-inch (25 cm) circle. Line 9-inch (23 cm) pie plate with 1 of the circles; spoon in vegetable mixture. Lightly brush pastry edge with some of the milk. Top with remaining pastry; trim edge. Using tines of fork, press edges together to seal and crimp. Brush top with remaining milk; cut steam vents in top.

Bake on bottom rack in 400°F (200°C) oven until golden, about 40 minutes. Let stand for 5 minutes before cutting. *(Make-ahead: Let cool. Cover and refrigerate for up to 2 days. Loosely cover with foil; reheat in 350°F/180°C oven for 1¼ hours.)*

Makes 6 servings. PER SERVING: about 431 cal, 11 g pro, 20 g total fat (7 g sat. fat), 54 g carb, 8 g fibre, 32 mg chol, 1,051 mg sodium. % RDI: 8% calcium, 29% iron, 44% vit A, 103% vit C, 59% folate.

best **TIPS** ever

Herbs and spices are pantry staples that can liven up all sorts of dishes, but their bright flavours dull over time. For best results, buy spices in small amounts and store them for up to six months in airtight containers. Make sure they're in a cool, dark place – heat, humidity and light can weaken their potency quickly. Buy new herbs and spices often to keep your recipes vibrant.

Stroganoff Toss for Two
Budget-friendly ground beef seasoned with caraway and paprika is a taste sensation. This recipe can easily be doubled if you have a larger group at the table.

8 oz (225 g) **lean ground beef**

1 tsp **vegetable oil**

3 cups quartered **mushrooms**

1 **onion,** chopped

2 cloves **garlic,** minced

2 tsp **sweet paprika**

½ tsp **salt**

½ tsp **pepper**

½ tsp **caraway seeds,** crushed

½ cup **beef broth**

1 tbsp **wine vinegar**

½ cup **light sour cream**

1 tbsp **prepared horseradish**

4 cups **curly broad egg noodles**

3 tbsp chopped **fresh parsley**

In nonstick skillet, cook beef, breaking up with spoon, until no longer pink. Drain off any fat. Remove and set aside.

Add oil to pan; cook mushrooms, onion, garlic, paprika, salt, pepper and caraway seeds over medium heat, stirring often, until mushrooms are softened, about 8 minutes.

Stir in broth and vinegar. Return beef to pan. Remove from heat. Stir in sour cream and horseradish.

Meanwhile, in pot of boiling salted water, cook noodles until almost tender, about 8 minutes. Drain and return to pot. Add beef mixture and parsley; toss to coat.

Makes 2 servings. PER SERVING: about 696 cal, 42 g pro, 26 g total fat (9 g sat. fat), 75 g carb, 7 g fibre, 139 mg chol, 1,417 mg sodium, 1,153 mg potassium. % RDI: 18% calcium, 56% iron, 19% vit A, 27% vit C, 117% folate.

Sage Apple Pork Burgers With Caramelized Onions

Not your average backyard fare, these thick, juicy burgers, dressed up with lettuce and thinly sliced apple, are fancy enough for casual entertaining. And since you can make the patties ahead, they might become a weeknight grilling favourite too.

1 **egg**

¼ cup **apple juice**

2 **green onions,** chopped

¼ cup **dried bread crumbs**

1 tbsp finely chopped **fresh sage**
   (or ½ tsp dried)

½ tsp each **salt** and **pepper**

1 lb (450 g) **lean ground pork**

4 **onion buns** or hamburger buns

4 leaves **leaf lettuce**

1 **red-skinned apple,** thinly sliced

CARAMELIZED ONIONS:

1 tbsp **vegetable oil**

1 large **onion,** thinly sliced

1 tbsp **granulated sugar**

1 tbsp **wine vinegar**

¼ tsp each **salt** and **pepper**

In bowl, beat egg with apple juice. Stir in green onions, bread crumbs, sage, salt and pepper; mix in pork. Shape into four ½-inch (1 cm) thick patties. *(Make-ahead: Cover and refrigerate for up to 6 hours. Or layer between waxed paper in airtight container and freeze for up to 1 month; thaw in refrigerator.)*

CARAMELIZED ONIONS: In skillet, heat oil over medium-high heat; fry onion, stirring occasionally, until starting to turn golden, about 8 minutes. Sprinkle with sugar and vinegar; cook over medium heat, stirring occasionally, until deep golden, about 10 minutes. Sprinkle with salt and pepper.

Meanwhile, place patties on greased grill over medium-high heat; close lid and grill, turning once, until instant-read thermometer inserted sideways into several reads 160°F (71°C), about 10 minutes. Cut buns in half; place, cut sides down, on grill and toast until golden, 1 to 2 minutes.

Sandwich lettuce, apple, patties and caramelized onions in buns.

Makes 4 servings. PER SERVING: about 523 cal, 30 g pro, 21 g total fat (6 g sat. fat), 53 g carb, 6 g fibre, 121 mg chol, 906 mg sodium. % RDI: 12% calcium, 30% iron, 5% vit A, 20% vit C, 39% folate.

quick pork mains

Pork Katsu

These crunchy cutlets, topped with a drizzle of savoury-sweet sauce, are Japanese-style comfort food at its best. Serve them with steamed rice and a simple green vegetable for a satisfying dinner.

4 **boneless pork loin centre chops**
  (1½ lb/675 g total)
¼ tsp each **salt** and **pepper**
1 **egg**
2 tbsp **all-purpose flour**
1½ cups **panko** (see Tip, below)
Vegetable oil for frying
¼ cup **ketchup**
2 tbsp **Worcestershire sauce**

Between plastic wrap, pound pork with meat mallet or bottom of heavy skillet to about ½-inch (1 cm) thickness. Sprinkle with salt and pepper. Whisk egg with 1 tbsp water. Dip pork into flour to coat; shake off excess. Dip into egg mixture, letting excess drip off. Dip into panko, patting to coat evenly.

In deep skillet, heat 1 inch (2.5 cm) oil over medium heat; cook pork, in batches, until juices run clear when pork is pierced and just a hint of pink remains inside, 6 to 8 minutes.

Meanwhile, whisk ketchup with Worcestershire sauce. Serve with pork.

Makes 4 to 6 servings. PER EACH OF 6 SERVINGS: about 281 cal, 27 g pro, 14 g total fat (4 g sat. fat), 11 g carb, 1 g fibre, 92 mg chol, 340 mg sodium, 485 mg potassium. % RDI: 2% calcium, 11% iron, 2% vit A, 5% vit C, 7% folate.

best **TIPS** ever

Panko is the Japanese name for large, fluffy dried bread crumbs. Bags of them are easy to find in Asian grocery stores, and an increasing number of supermarkets are carrying them. Panko adds a delicious crunch to any sort of breaded food.

Toasted Black Peppercorn & Cumin Pork Tenderloin

Toasting spices brings out their complex flavours and aromas. The hint of brown sugar in the spice rub helps create a deliciously caramelized crust on the pork.

1 tbsp **black peppercorns**

1 tbsp **cumin seeds**

2 tsp packed **brown sugar**

½ tsp **salt**

2 **pork tenderloins** (about 2 lb/900 g total)

1 tbsp **extra-virgin olive oil**

½ cup **whipping cream (35%)**

⅓ cup **cognac** or brandy

2 tsp **Dijon mustard**

In dry small skillet, toast peppercorns and cumin seeds over medium heat, stirring often, until fragrant, about 5 minutes. Let cool.

In spice grinder or using mortar and pestle, finely grind peppercorns and cumin seeds. Stir in brown sugar and salt. Rub all over pork, pressing to adhere. *(Make-ahead: Cover and refrigerate for up to 2 hours.)*

In large ovenproof skillet, heat oil over medium-high heat; sear pork on all sides until well browned, about 6 minutes.

Roast in 400°F (200°C) oven until juices run clear when pork is pierced and just a hint of pink remains inside, about 25 minutes. Transfer to cutting board and tent with foil; let stand for 5 minutes, reserving accumulated juices. Carve into 1-inch (2.5 cm) thick slices; transfer to platter.

Meanwhile, in small saucepan, whisk together cream, cognac and mustard; gently boil until reduced to about ½ cup, about 8 minutes. Stir in accumulated pork juices; pour over pork.

Makes 6 to 8 servings. PER EACH OF 8 SERVINGS: about 228 cal, 28 g pro, 10 g total fat (5 g sat. fat), 3 g carb, trace fibre, 86 mg chol, 224 mg sodium. % RDI: 3% calcium, 16% iron, 5% vit A, 2% vit C, 2% folate.

Roasted Pork Tenderloin With Red Onion Gravy

Roasted root vegetables, such as potatoes, are the perfect side for this tenderloin. Begin roasting them on a rimmed baking sheet 15 minutes before starting the pork. Then nestle the pork next to the vegetables when you transfer it to the oven.

1 lb (450 g) **pork tenderloin**

1 tbsp **extra-virgin olive oil**

2 tsp finely chopped **fresh rosemary**

¼ tsp each **salt** and **pepper**

1 tbsp **unsalted butter**

1 large **red onion,** finely chopped

1 **bay leaf**

1 clove **garlic,** minced

½ cup **red wine**

1 tbsp **all-purpose flour**

1 cup **sodium-reduced chicken broth**

Rub pork with 1 tsp of the oil, the rosemary, salt and pepper. In large skillet, heat remaining oil over medium-high heat; brown pork all over, about 4 minutes.

Transfer to rimmed baking sheet; roast in 425°F (220°C) oven until juices run clear when pork is pierced and just a hint of pink remains inside, 10 to 15 minutes. Tent with foil; let stand for 8 minutes before carving.

Meanwhile, in same skillet, melt butter over medium-low heat; cover and cook onion and bay leaf, stirring occasionally, for 15 minutes. Add garlic; cook until onion is caramelized and softened, 2 to 3 minutes.

Stir in wine and increase heat to medium-high; cook, scraping up browned bits, until reduced by half.

Add flour; cook, stirring, for 1 minute. Whisk in broth and bring to boil; reduce heat and simmer until thickened, 2 to 3 minutes. Add water, 1 tbsp at a time, to thin gravy if desired. Discard bay leaf. Serve sauce with pork.

Makes 4 servings. PER SERVING: about 247 cal, 27 g pro, 9 g total fat (3 g sat. fat), 11 g carb, 2 g fibre, 69 mg chol, 347 mg sodium, 540 mg potassium. % RDI: 3% calcium, 12% iron, 3% vit A, 8% vit C, 10% folate.

easy dinner for 4

Radicchio, Spinach & Walnut Salad

This colourful combination of bitter radicchio, tender baby spinach and crunchy walnuts creates an intriguing mix of textures and flavours. Walnut oil is available in most supermarkets, or you can make your own by following the tip below.

Half head **radicchio,**
   torn in bite-size pieces

4 cups **fresh baby spinach**

½ cup **walnut halves,** toasted

WALNUT DRESSING:

2 tbsp **canola oil** or vegetable oil

1 tbsp **walnut oil** (see Tip, below)

1 tbsp **sherry vinegar**

½ tsp **Dijon mustard**

Pinch each **salt** and **pepper**

WALNUT DRESSING: Whisk together canola oil, walnut oil, vinegar, mustard, salt and pepper.

In large bowl, toss radicchio with spinach. Break walnuts into pieces; add to bowl along with dressing. Toss to coat.

Makes 6 servings. PER SERVING: about 133 cal, 2 g pro, 13 g total fat (1 g sat. fat), 3 g carb, 1 g fibre, 0 mg chol, 25 mg sodium. % RDI: 3% calcium, 6% iron, 19% vit A, 12% vit C, 26% folate.

best **TIPS** ever

Homemade walnut-flavoured oil isn't as strong-tasting as commercial walnut oil, but it's nice on this salad. To make it, increase the canola or vegetable oil to 3 tbsp and omit the walnut oil. In skillet, heat oil over medium heat; cook walnut halves, stirring, until golden, about 3 minutes. With slotted spoon, transfer nuts to paper towel–lined plate; let nuts and oil cool. Strain oil through fine sieve. *(Make-ahead: Cover and refrigerate for up to 24 hours.)* Prepare salad and dressing as directed.

Sweet Potato, Celeriac & Apple Purée

This purée is a refreshing side dish for turkey or pork.

Half large **celeriac,** peeled and cut in
   1½-inch (4 cm) cubes
2 lb (900 g) **sweet potatoes,** peeled and chopped
3 tbsp **unsalted butter**
1 **Golden Delicious apple,** peeled and sliced
¼ tsp grated **nutmeg**

In large pot of boiling salted water, cover and cook celeriac for 5 minutes.

Add sweet potatoes; cook, covered, until vegetables are tender, 10 to 12 minutes. Reserving 1 cup of the cooking liquid, drain; return to low heat for 1 minute to dry vegetables.

Meanwhile, in small skillet, melt 1 tbsp of the butter over medium heat. Stir in apple and nutmeg; cook, stirring often, until softened, about 8 minutes.

In batches in food processor, purée potato mixture with apple until smooth; transfer to bowl. Stir in reserved cooking liquid and remaining butter. *(Make-ahead: Refrigerate in airtight container for up to 2 days. Reheat to serve.)*

Makes 6 to 8 servings. PER EACH OF 8 SERVINGS: about 135 cal, 2 g pro, 5 g total fat (3 g sat. fat), 23 g carb, 3 g fibre, 11 mg chol, 453 mg sodium, 328 mg potassium. % RDI: 4% calcium, 6% iron, 161% vit A, 25% vit C, 4% folate.

Light Berry Fool

Fools are old-fashioned desserts made of fruit folded into whipped cream. This one is lightened up with a bit of thick yogurt.

1 cup **Balkan-style plain yogurt**
¾ cup **whipping cream (35%)**
2 tbsp **granulated sugar**
Dash **vanilla**
1 cup drained thawed **frozen mixed berries**
Fresh mint leaves

Line sieve with cheesecloth; set over bowl. Add yogurt; refrigerate until slightly thickened, about 1 hour. Transfer drained yogurt to large bowl.

In separate bowl, whip together cream, sugar and vanilla; fold into yogurt.

Fold in berries (see Tip, below), leaving streaks. Spoon into stemmed glasses; garnish with mint.

Makes 4 servings. PER SERVING: about 246 cal, 3 g pro, 19 g total fat (12 g sat. fat), 16 g carb, 2 g fibre, 68 mg chol, 35 mg sodium, 165 mg potassium. % RDI: 10% calcium, 2% iron, 20% vit A, 18% vit C, 5% folate.

best TIPS ever

This fool gets its light texture through folding, or gently combining a light, airy mixture (in this case, whipped cream) with a heavier mixture (drained yogurt). Folding ensures the air bubbles don't break down and the mixture doesn't deflate or lose volume. To fold, place the light mixture on top of the heavy mixture. Using rubber spatula and starting at back of bowl, gently cut down through mixtures. Cut across bottom of bowl to front. Cut up front to top and fold over. Rotate bowl one-quarter turn after each fold. Gently fold just until combined (not overmixed) to prevent deflation.

Tofu & Vegetable Skewers With Peanut Sauce

Mild tofu always benefits from the addition of a savoury sauce. Here, a salty-sweet peanut sauce gives the skewers a scrumptious flavour boost.

1 pkg (350 g) **extra-firm tofu**

2 cups **snow peas,** trimmed

2 cups **cherry tomatoes**

2 cups small **mushrooms**

2 tbsp **extra-virgin olive oil**

¼ tsp each **salt** and **pepper**

2 **green onions,** sliced

PEANUT SAUCE:

½ cup **smooth peanut butter**

¼ cup **soy sauce**

2 tbsp **ketchup**

2 tbsp **lemon juice**

2 cloves **garlic,** minced

PEANUT SAUCE: In bowl, whisk together peanut butter, ½ cup warm water, soy sauce, ketchup, lemon juice and garlic. Set aside ¾ cup.

Pat tofu dry. Cut in half horizontally; cut in half lengthwise. Cut crosswise into sixths to make 24 pieces total. Add to remaining peanut sauce; let stand for 10 minutes. Thread onto 4 skewers.

Meanwhile, in separate bowl, toss together snow peas, tomatoes, mushrooms, oil, salt and pepper. Alternately thread vegetables onto 8 skewers.

Place tofu and vegetable skewers on greased grill over medium-high heat; close lid and grill, turning once, until tofu is browned and vegetables are tender-crisp, about 10 minutes. To serve, drizzle with reserved peanut sauce; sprinkle with green onions.

Makes 4 servings. PER SERVING: about 303 cal, 17 g pro, 22 g total fat (4 g sat. fat), 15 g carb, 4 g fibre, 0 mg chol, 908 mg sodium. % RDI: 15% calcium, 26% iron, 8% vit A, 50% vit C, 29% folate.

easy grilled mains

Grilled Pork Chops & Apple Rings

These grilled apple rings are sweet and juicy – perfect with simple spiced pork chops.

4 **pork loin centre chops** (1¼ lb/565 g total)
½ tsp **salt**
¼ tsp each **ground cumin, ground ginger** and **cinnamon**
Pinch **cayenne pepper**
2 **Golden Delicious apples**
2 tsp **maple syrup** or liquid honey

Trim fat from pork chops; slash edges at ½-inch (1 cm) intervals to prevent curling. Combine salt, cumin, ginger, cinnamon and cayenne pepper; rub on both sides of chops.

Place on greased grill or in grill pan over medium-high heat; close lid and grill, turning once, until juices run clear when pork is pierced and just a hint of pink remains inside, 8 to 10 minutes.

Meanwhile, cut apples into ½-inch (1 cm) thick rings. Add to grill with pork chops; grill, turning once, until grill-marked and tender, about 4 minutes. Brush with maple syrup. Arrange apples and pork chops on platter.

Makes 4 servings. PER SERVING: about 198 cal, 21 g pro, 7 g total fat (3 g sat. fat), 13 g carb, 2 g fibre, 58 mg chol, 336 mg sodium. % RDI: 3% calcium, 8% iron, 7% vit C, 2% folate.

Whole Grilled Trout With Lemon Parsley Butter

The key to grilling whole fish is to grease the grill (not the fish) so the skin doesn't stick.

2 **whole trout** (about 1 lb/450 g each), cleaned
1½ tsp **sea salt** or salt
½ tsp **pepper**
1 **lemon,** sliced
Half bunch **fresh parsley**
1 bunch **fresh thyme** (optional)

LEMON PARSLEY BUTTER:
¼ cup **unsalted butter,** softened
1 tbsp chopped **fresh parsley**
2 tsp grated **lemon zest**
1 tsp **lemon juice**
Pinch each **salt** and **pepper**

LEMON PARSLEY BUTTER: Mash together butter, parsley, lemon zest and juice, salt and pepper. Scrape onto plastic wrap; shape into 1-inch (2.5 cm) diameter log and wrap tightly. Refrigerate until firm, about 1 hour. (Make-ahead: Refrigerate for up to 24 hours.)

Sprinkle trout cavities with half each of the salt and pepper. Stuff cavities with lemon slices, parsley, and thyme (if using); skewer closed. Sprinkle fish with remaining salt and pepper.

Place on well-greased grill over medium-high heat; close lid and grill, turning once, until fish flakes easily when tested, about 10 minutes per inch (2.5 cm) of thickness. Transfer to platter.

Slice butter into ½-inch (1 cm) thick rounds and serve with fish.

Makes 6 servings. PER SERVING: about 210 cal, 20 g pro, 14 g total fat (7 g sat. fat), 3 g carb, 1 g fibre, 75 mg chol, 425 mg sodium. % RDI: 8% calcium, 6% iron, 18% vit A, 40% vit C, 13% folate.

best **TIPS** ever

To serve a cooked whole fish, run knife along backbone to cut through skin; pull off skin, then ease knife along between flesh and bone on top side. Ease off top fillet; cut into portions. Turn fish and repeat.

Chipotle Grilled Chicken

This chicken has a delicious bite thanks to the chipotle peppers (smoked ripe red jalapeños), which are available canned in adobo sauce in the Mexican section of many grocery stores and specialty food shops.

6 **chicken breasts** or legs (about
   3 lb/1.35 kg total)
1 can (5½ oz/156 mL) **tomato paste**
¾ cup **dry white wine** or
   chicken broth
2 **canned chipotle peppers in
   adobo sauce**
1 tbsp **adobo sauce**
2 cloves **garlic,** minced
¾ tsp **salt**
½ tsp **pepper**

Starting at thicker end of chicken breasts or thigh end of legs and gripping with paper towel, pull skin downward away from flesh to remove; discard skin. Place chicken in large glass bowl.

In blender or food processor, purée together tomato paste, wine, chipotle peppers, adobo sauce, garlic, salt and pepper until smooth; pour over chicken, turning to coat. Cover and refrigerate for 4 hours. *(Make-ahead: Refrigerate for up to 1 day.)*

Place chicken, bone side down, on greased grill over medium heat; baste with marinade. Close lid and grill, turning occasionally, until breasts are no longer pink inside or juices run clear when thickest parts of thighs are pierced, about 45 minutes.

Makes 6 servings. PER SERVING: about 209 cal, 37 g pro, 3 g total fat (1 g sat. fat), 7 g carb, 1 g fibre, 92 mg chol, 431 mg sodium. % RDI: 2% calcium, 12% iron, 11% vit A, 22% vit C, 4% folate.

From top: Ginger Soy Salmon Fillets (opposite) and Orange Rice (page 36)

Ginger Soy Salmon Fillets
Whether you choose to make the weeknight-friendly fillets or a splashy weekend-worthy side of salmon, this fresh marinade really complements the rich fish.

6 **skin-on salmon fillets** (6 oz/170 g each)
¼ cup **soy sauce**
2 tbsp chopped **fresh mint**
2 tbsp grated **fresh ginger**
2 tbsp **unseasoned rice vinegar**
1 tbsp **sesame oil**
Lemon wedges

Place salmon in shallow dish. Stir together soy sauce, mint, ginger, vinegar and sesame oil; pour over salmon. Cover and refrigerate for 15 minutes.

Place salmon, skin side down, on greased grill over medium heat; brush with any remaining marinade. Close lid and grill until fish flakes easily when tested, about 10 minutes. Serve with lemon wedges.

Makes 6 servings. PER SERVING: about 246 cal, 24 g pro, 15 g total fat (3 g sat. fat), 2 g carb, trace fibre, 66 mg chol, 664 mg sodium. % RDI: 2% calcium, 5% iron, 2% vit A, 10% vit C, 17% folate.

change it up
Ginger Soy Side of Salmon: Substitute 1 side of salmon (about 2 lb/900 g) for the fillets; marinate as directed. Grill until fish flakes easily when tested, about 20 minutes.

easy salmon dinner

Braised Bok Choy
Delicate bok choy is a no-fuss, healthy side dish that cooks up in no time.

¼ cup **sodium-reduced chicken broth**

1 tsp **cornstarch**

¼ tsp **salt**

Pinch each **granulated sugar** and **pepper**

2 tbsp **vegetable oil**

1 clove **garlic,** thinly sliced

1 lb (450 g) **baby bok choy,** halved lengthwise

1 tsp **sesame oil**

½ tsp **sesame seeds,** toasted

Whisk together chicken broth, cornstarch, salt, sugar and pepper; set aside.

In wok or large skillet, heat oil over medium-high heat; stir-fry garlic for 5 seconds. Add bok choy; stir-fry until bright green, about 2 minutes. Cover and steam, stirring occasionally, until stalks are tender-crisp, 4 to 8 minutes.

Stir in broth mixture and bring to boil; reduce heat and simmer, uncovered, until almost no liquid remains, about 2 minutes. Transfer to plate; drizzle with sesame oil. Sprinkle with sesame seeds.

Makes 4 servings. PER SERVING: about 60 cal, 1 g pro, 5 g total fat (trace sat. fat), 2 g carb, 1 g fibre, 0 mg chol, 149 mg sodium. % RDI: 7% calcium, 6% iron, 35% vit A, 35% vit C, 15% folate.

Orange Rice
Why eat plain rice when this orange-scented, carrot-studded version is so simple to make?

2⅔ cups **chicken broth**

1½ tsp grated **orange zest**

¼ tsp each **salt** and **pepper**

1⅓ cups **long-grain rice**

1 large **carrot,** grated

In saucepan, combine broth, orange zest, salt and pepper; bring to boil.

Stir in rice and carrot. Cover, reduce heat and simmer until rice is tender and liquid is absorbed, about 25 minutes. Fluff with fork.

Makes 4 servings. PER SERVING: about 243 cal, 6 g pro, 1 g total fat (trace sat. fat), 51 g carb, 2 g fibre, 0 mg chol, 775 mg sodium, 118 mg potassium. % RDI: 3% calcium, 4% iron, 40% vit A, 3% vit C, 4% folate.

Mango Sorbet With Macerated Strawberries

Making sorbet by hand is very straightforward, but you can freeze the mango mixture in your ice-cream maker if you like; just follow the manufacturer's instructions.

1 cup **granulated sugar**

1 **ripe mango,** peeled, pitted and cut in chunks
(see Tips, below)

¼ cup **lemon juice**

MACERATED STRAWBERRIES:

⅓ cup **orange-flavoured liqueur** or orange juice

⅓ cup **orange juice**

2 tsp **liquid honey**

½ tsp grated **lemon zest**

1 **ripe mango,** peeled, pitted and cut in chunks

2 cups **strawberries,** hulled and quartered

MACERATED STRAWBERRIES: In nonreactive bowl, combine liqueur, orange juice, honey and lemon zest. Add mango and strawberries; stir gently. Let stand at room temperature for 1 hour. *(Make-ahead: Cover and refrigerate for up to 6 hours.)*

In saucepan, bring sugar and 1 cup water to boil, stirring until dissolved. Reduce heat; simmer for 1 minute. Let cool. In food processor, purée together mango, sugar syrup and lemon juice until smooth. Press through fine sieve into bowl. Pour into shallow metal pan; freeze until almost firm, 3 to 4 hours.

Break into chunks. Transfer to food processor; purée until smooth. Freeze in airtight container until firm, about 1 hour. *(Make-ahead: Freeze for up to 1 week.)*

Serve with macerated strawberries.

Makes 6 servings. PER SERVING: about 260 cal, 1 g pro, 1 g total fat (trace sat. fat), 59 g carb, 2 g fibre, 0 mg chol, 5 mg sodium, 234 mg potassium. % RDI: 2% calcium, 3% iron, 6% vit A, 103% vit C, 14% folate.

best **TIPS** ever

• Canadian supermarkets most often stock "apple mangoes," a roundish variety from Central and South America and the West Indies. Mottled yellow and red skin, often with a bit of green, signals ripeness. For this sorbet, choose a redder, softer mango. The stem end should be fragrant; an unbruised mango with sap oozing from the stem will have the best flavour.

• Here's a foolproof method for cubing a mango: Cut off the stem end to create a flat bottom. Then, using a potato peeler, peel off half of the skin. Hold the peeled side with a paper towel to prevent slipping and peel opposite side. Stand mango on flat bottom, then cut flesh off each wide side, down to but avoiding the pit. Place slices on cutting board; cube.

Stove-Top Macaroni & Cheese

This quick sauce comes together as the pasta cooks to make a dish that's heaps better than any boxed variety. For the best flavour, use extra-old Cheddar cheese.

2 tbsp **butter**

Half **onion,** diced

½ tsp **salt**

Pinch **cayenne pepper**

1 tbsp **all-purpose flour**

1½ cups **milk**

2 tsp **Dijon mustard**

1¼ cups shredded **old Cheddar cheese** or extra-old Cheddar cheese

2½ cups **small shell pasta** or elbow macaroni (about 12 oz/340 g)

In large saucepan, melt butter over medium heat; cook onion, salt and cayenne pepper, stirring occasionally, until softened, about 6 minutes.

Stir in flour; cook, stirring, for 2 minutes. Gradually whisk in milk and mustard; cook, whisking, until bubbly and thickened, 10 minutes. Stir in Cheddar cheese until smooth.

Meanwhile, in large pot of boiling salted water, cook pasta according to package instructions until al dente. Drain and add to sauce; stir to coat.

Makes 4 servings. PER SERVING: about 569 cal, 23 g pro, 21 g total fat (12 g sat. fat), 71 g carb, 4 g fibre, 60 mg chol, 840 mg sodium. % RDI: 35% calcium, 26% iron, 19% vit A, 85% folate.

easy cheesy mains

Caprese Pizza With Bacon This grilled pizza has all the iconic flavours of a Caprese salad – fresh mozzarella cheese, tomatoes and basil – on a crisp, slightly smoky crust.

6 slices **bacon**

4 oz (115 g) **fresh mozzarella cheese** or
   large bocconcini cheese

1 lb (450 g) **pizza dough**

2 tsp **extra-virgin olive oil**

½ cup **Basil Pesto** (opposite)

1 **tomato,** sliced in ¼-inch (5 mm) thick rounds

2 tbsp sliced **fresh basil**

Cut bacon slices in half. In skillet, cook bacon over medium heat until almost crisp but still slightly chewy, about 8 minutes. Transfer to paper towel–lined plate; set aside.

Drain mozzarella cheese; pat dry (see Tip, below). Cut into ¼-inch (5 mm) thick rounds. Arrange on separate paper towel–lined tray; pat rounds dry.

On lightly floured surface, roll out dough into 16- x 12-inch (40 x 30 cm) rectangle; transfer to lightly floured pizza peel or inverted baking sheet.

Brush with oil. Place, oiled side down, directly on greased grill over medium heat. Grill, uncovered and watching carefully to avoid charring, until bubbles form on top and grill-marked underneath, 3 to 6 minutes.

Flip crust; close lid and grill just until set, about 1 minute. Transfer to lightly floured pizza peel or inverted baking sheet. Reduce heat to medium-low.

Spread with pesto; top with tomato, bacon and cheese. Slide pizza back onto grill. Close lid and grill until bubbly and underside is browned, 3 to 8 minutes. Sprinkle with basil.

Makes 8 slices. PER SLICE: about 301 cal, 11 g pro, 17 g total fat (5 g sat. fat), 27 g carb, 2 g fibre, 20 mg chol, 520 mg sodium, 187 mg potassium. % RDI: 17% calcium, 15% iron, 7% vit A, 5% vit C, 25% folate.

best
TIPS
ever

Fresh mozzarella, whether it's made into large balls or small bocconcini, is packed in water (in small consumer tubs or big industrial ones at the deli counter) to keep it soft and moist. When you're cooking with this type of cheese, be sure to pat it dry to prevent it from making other ingredients soggy.

Basil Pesto This simple recipe tastes so fresh that you'll never buy premade pesto again – especially when you discover how well it freezes.

¼ cup **pine nuts**

2 cups packed **fresh basil leaves**

¼ tsp each **salt** and **pepper**

⅓ cup **extra-virgin olive oil**

½ cup grated **Parmesan cheese**

1 clove **garlic,** minced

In dry small skillet, toast pine nuts over medium heat, shaking pan often, until light golden, 3 to 5 minutes. Transfer to food processor; let cool.

Add basil, salt and pepper; finely chop together. With motor running, add oil in thin steady stream until puréed. Pulse in Parmesan cheese and garlic. *(Make-ahead: Refrigerate in airtight container for up to 3 days or freeze for up to 6 months.)*

Makes about 1 cup. PER 1 TBSP: about 69 cal, 2 g pro, 7 g total fat (1 g sat. fat), 1 g carb, trace fibre, 3 mg chol, 84 mg sodium, 42 mg potassium. % RDI: 4% calcium, 3% iron, 3% vit A, 2% vit C, 2% folate.

Traditional Three-Cheese Fondue
Serve this rich Gorgonzola-laced fondue with cubed baguette and sour gherkins.

1 clove **garlic,** halved

2½ cups **dry white wine**

1 lb (450 g) **Emmental cheese,**
   shredded (4 cups)

1 lb (450 g) **Gruyère cheese,**
   shredded (4 cups)

3 tbsp **cornstarch**

Pinch each **cayenne pepper** and **nutmeg**

8 oz (225 g) **Gorgonzola cheese,** cubed

2 tbsp **kirsch,** eau-de-vie or Calvados

Vigorously rub inside of stoveproof fondue pot or 12-cup (3 L) saucepan with cut sides of garlic; discard garlic. Pour in wine; bring to simmer over medium heat.

In bowl, toss together Emmental and Gruyère cheeses, cornstarch, cayenne pepper and nutmeg. Using wooden spoon and stirring in figure-eight motion, stir cheese mixture into wine in 3 additions, returning to simmer and stirring until smooth before each addition.

Stir in Gorgonzola cheese and kirsch; cook, stirring, until bubbly and smooth.

Place over medium-low heat of fondue burner on table; adjust heat as necessary to maintain low simmer and stir often to prevent sticking.

Makes 6 to 8 servings. PER EACH OF 8 SERVINGS: about 600 cal, 39 g pro, 45 g total fat (27 g sat. fat), 6 g carb, 0 g fibre, 141 mg chol, 783 mg sodium. % RDI: 111% calcium, 3% iron, 39% vit A, 12% folate.

Cornmeal-Crusted Pickerel BLT

Here's a heavenly hybrid of a crispy fish sandwich and a BLT. Homemade tartar sauce is utterly delicious on this creation, but store-bought works if you're short on time.

4 slices **bacon** (optional)

4 **skinless pickerel fillets** (1 lb/450 g total)

¼ tsp each **salt** and **pepper**

⅓ cup **cornmeal**

1 tbsp **vegetable oil**

4 **oval buns,** halved

4 leaves **romaine lettuce**

2 **plum tomatoes,** sliced

TARTAR SAUCE:

⅓ cup **light mayonnaise**

2 tbsp chopped **cornichons** (sour gherkins) or sweet green relish

1 tbsp chopped rinsed drained **capers** (optional)

1 tsp **lemon juice**

Pinch each **salt** and **pepper**

TARTAR SAUCE: Mix together mayonnaise, cornichons, capers (if using), lemon juice, salt and pepper. Set aside in refrigerator.

Cut bacon (if using) in half crosswise. In nonstick skillet, fry until crisp; transfer to paper towel–lined plate. Drain fat from pan.

Meanwhile, sprinkle fish with salt and pepper. In shallow dish, press fish into cornmeal, turning to coat.

In same skillet, heat oil over medium heat; fry fish, turning once, until crisp, golden and flakes easily when tested, 6 to 8 minutes. Sandwich fish in buns along with tartar sauce, lettuce, tomatoes and bacon.

Makes 4 servings. PER SERVING: about 425 cal, 29 g pro, 14 g total fat (2 g sat. fat), 44 g carb, 3 g fibre, 104 mg chol, 779 mg sodium, 649 mg potassium. % RDI: 18% calcium, 29% iron, 16% vit A, 13% vit C, 49% folate.

more sandwiches for dinner

Poached Eggs on Spinach Feta Toast

Who doesn't love breakfast for dinner? If you don't have a large round loaf of sourdough, just divide the spinach mixture among 8 regular slices of bread for this open-faced sandwich.

½ cup thawed **frozen spinach**
(see Tip, below)

½ cup crumbled **feta cheese**

½ cup finely chopped **green onions**

2 tsp chopped **fresh oregano**
(or ½ tsp dried)

1 small clove **garlic,** minced

¼ tsp each **salt** and **pepper**

3 tbsp **olive oil**

4 thick slices **sourdough bread,**
toasted

1 tbsp **vinegar**

8 **eggs**

Finely chop spinach; squeeze out excess moisture. In bowl, stir together spinach, feta cheese, all but 2 tbsp of the green onions, the oregano, garlic and pinch each of the salt and pepper. Stir in olive oil; spread over bread. Bake on baking sheet in 350°F (180°C) oven until cheese is slightly softened, about 10 minutes.

Meanwhile, in deep skillet, heat 2 to 3 inches (5 to 8 cm) water over medium heat until simmering. Stir in vinegar. One at a time, crack eggs into small cup; gently slide into simmering water. Reduce heat to low; cook until whites are set and yolks are still soft, about 3 minutes. With slotted spoon, transfer to paper towel–lined tray.

Place 2 eggs on each toast; sprinkle with remaining salt, pepper and green onions.

Makes 4 servings. PER SERVING: about 398 cal, 19 g pro, 25 g total fat (8 g sat. fat), 23 g carb, 2 g fibre, 389 mg chol, 720 mg sodium, 260 mg potassium. % RDI: 19% calcium, 20% iron, 33% vit A, 3% vit C, 48% folate.

best **TIPS** ever

Cooked spinach is notoriously watery, especially when it has been frozen and thawed. To remove the maximum amount of liquid, drain the spinach in a fine-mesh sieve, then squeeze it by handfuls over the sink.

Braided Cheesy Beef Sandwich

Burger and pizza lovers will adore this saucy filling bundled up in pizza dough. The versatile, freeze-ahead meat mixture makes enough for four meals – try it in pasta sauce and sloppy joes.

2 tbsp **cornmeal**

1 lb (450 g) **pizza dough**

½ cup shredded **mild Cheddar cheese**

1 **egg,** beaten

FILLING:

2 tsp **vegetable oil**

1 **carrot,** grated

1 **zucchini,** grated

1 tsp **dried basil**

¼ tsp each **salt** and **pepper**

½ cup **chili sauce**

GROUND BEEF & SAUSAGE MIX:

1 lb (450 g) **mild Italian sausage,** casings removed and meat cut in bite-size pieces

3 lb (1.35 kg) **lean ground beef**

2 tbsp **vegetable oil**

3 **onions,** chopped

3 cloves **garlic,** minced

6 cups sliced **mushrooms** (1 lb/450 g)

1 cup **beef broth** (approx)

1 can (5½ oz/156 mL) **tomato paste**

GROUND BEEF & SAUSAGE MIX: In large saucepan, cook sausage and beef over medium-high heat, breaking up with spoon, until no longer pink, 10 minutes. Drain liquid into 2-cup glass measure; transfer meat to bowl. Set aside. Add oil to pan; cook onions, garlic and mushrooms over medium heat, stirring, until softened, 8 minutes. Skim fat off reserved liquid; add enough broth to make 2 cups. Stir into pan along with meat mixture and tomato paste. Bring to boil; reduce heat and simmer for 20 minutes. Measure 3 cups and set aside; save remainder for another use. *(Make-ahead: Freeze in airtight container for up to 2 weeks; thaw in refrigerator.)*

FILLING: In saucepan, heat oil over medium heat; cook carrot, zucchini, basil, salt and pepper, stirring, for 3 minutes. Add reserved meat mixture and chili sauce; cook, stirring occasionally, until liquid is evaporated, about 15 minutes.

Sprinkle cornmeal on greased large rimmed baking sheet. On floured surface, roll out pizza dough into 15- x 10-inch (38 x 25 cm) rectangle; transfer to baking sheet. Sprinkle Cheddar cheese in 4-inch (10 cm) wide strip lengthwise down centre of dough. Spoon filling over cheese.

Starting at corner of 1 long side and stopping about ½ inch (1 cm) before filling, make 10 diagonal cuts to form 1½-inch (4 cm) wide strips. Repeat on opposite side. Brush strips with some of the egg. Fold strips over filling, alternating sides to create braided top. Brush with remaining egg.

Bake in 425°F (220°C) oven for 5 minutes. Reduce heat to 400°F (200°C); bake until golden, about 15 minutes.

Makes 6 servings. PER SERVING: about 437 cal, 23 g pro, 17 g total fat (6 g sat. fat), 48 g carb, 5 g fibre, 80 mg chol, 962 mg sodium. % RDI: 10% calcium, 31% iron, 38% vit A, 17% vit C, 29% folate.

Salsa-Stuffed Muffin Meat Loaves

Black beans add fibre and bulk to these little Tex Mex–inspired loaves. Serve with mashed potatoes and green beans for a simple supper everyone will love.

½ cup **fresh whole wheat bread crumbs**

1 **green onion,** chopped

½ cup rinsed drained **canned black beans**

1½ tsp **chili powder**

½ tsp **pepper**

Pinch **salt**

1 **egg**

1 lb (450 g) **extra-lean ground beef**

⅓ cup **salsa**

½ cup shredded **Monterey Jack cheese** or
   Cheddar cheese

In large bowl, combine bread crumbs, green onion, black beans, chili powder, pepper, salt and egg. Mix in beef. Shape into 8 balls. Place each in lightly greased muffin cup.

With spoon, make well in centre of each; fill with salsa and sprinkle with Monterey Jack cheese.

Bake in 400°F (200°C) oven until instant-read thermometer inserted into centre of several reads 160°F (71°C), about 15 minutes.

Makes 4 servings. PER SERVING: about 335 cal, 32 g pro, 15 g total fat (7 g sat. fat), 16 g carb, 4 g fibre, 122 mg chol, 482 mg sodium, 543 mg potassium. % RDI: 15% calcium, 28% iron, 8% vit A, 3% vit C, 19% folate.

Creamy Polenta With Herbs

Comforting, smooth and creamy, this polenta makes a stick-to-your-ribs side or vegetarian main.

3 cups **vegetable broth**

3 cups **milk**

½ tsp each **dried oregano** and **salt**

¼ tsp **dried basil**

1 cup **cornmeal**

¼ cup grated **Parmesan cheese** or
　Romano cheese

½ cup shredded **Edam cheese,**
　Muenster cheese or Cheddar cheese

In saucepan, heat broth, milk, oregano, salt and basil over medium-high heat until bubbles form around edge. Gradually whisk in cornmeal until thickened.

Reduce heat to low; cook, stirring often, until polenta is thick enough to mound on spoon, about 10 minutes. Stir in Parmesan cheese. Spoon into shallow bowls; sprinkle with Edam cheese.

Makes 6 to 8 servings. PER EACH OF 8 SERVINGS: about 155 cal, 8 g pro, 5 g total fat (3 g sat. fat), 19 g carb, 1 g fibre, 16 mg chol, 552 mg sodium. % RDI: 19% calcium, 3% iron, 8% vit A, 1% vit C, 5% folate.

Leafy Avocado Radish Salad

Radishes add a nice peppery bite to this cool green salad. Lime zest and juice brighten the flavours.

2 tbsp **extra-virgin olive oil**

1 tbsp grated **lime zest** or
　lemon zest

2 tbsp **lime juice** or
　lemon juice

¼ tsp each **salt** and **pepper**

6 cups chopped **leaf lettuce**

1 **avocado,** peeled and cubed

⅓ cup grated **radish**

⅓ cup sliced **red onion**

In bowl, whisk together oil, lime zest, lime juice, salt and pepper. Toss in lettuce, avocado, radish and onion.

Makes 4 servings. PER SERVING: about 156 cal, 2 g pro, 14 g total fat (2 g sat. fat), 8 g carb, 5 g fibre, 0 mg chol, 167 mg sodium, 394 mg potassium. % RDI: 3% calcium, 6% iron, 41% vit A, 35% vit C, 30% folate.

best TIPS ever

If you need just half an avocado, save the side with the pit intact and rub the cut flesh with a bit of lemon juice. Cover it tightly with plastic wrap and keep it in the refrigerator. To store guacamole or avocado-based sauces, add the pit if you like (some people swear by this method). Place plastic wrap directly on the surface and refrigerate it to keep the pretty green shade from turning muddy.

Lime Squash Cool and
refreshing, this nonalcoholic beverage looks great in a pitcher with plenty of ice – and tastes even better.

1¼ cups **lime juice** (about 6 limes)
⅓ cup **liquid honey**
2 bottles (750 mL each) **sparkling water**
Ice cubes

In glass measure, microwave lime juice with honey on high for 30 seconds; whisk until honey is dissolved. Let cool.

In pitcher, pour sparkling water over ice cubes; stir in lime mixture.

Makes 8 servings. PER SERVING: about 53 cal, trace pro, 0 g total fat (0 g sat. fat), 15 g carb, 0 g fibre, 0 mg chol, 3 mg sodium. % RDI: 3% calcium, 1% iron, 20% vit C, 2% folate.

Nectar-Sweet Pineapple
Fresh pineapple is a luscious dessert on its own, but with a drizzle of lemon juice and honey, it's simply divine.

8 slices **fresh golden pineapple**
2 tbsp **lemon juice**
2 tbsp **liquid honey**

Drizzle pineapple with lemon juice and honey.

Makes 4 servings. PER SERVING: about 88 cal, 1 g pro, 1 g total fat (0 g sat. fat), 23 g carb, 1 g fibre, 0 mg chol, 3 mg sodium. % RDI: 1% calcium, 4% iron, 32% vit C, 6% folate.

weekend dinners

Chicken Chorizo Paella

This easy paella has wonderful authentic flavour. You need only 1 tsp of tomato paste, so spoon evenly spaced tablespoonfuls of the leftovers onto plastic wrap. Roll up and twist between portions; freeze in an airtight container for up to a month. To use, just cut off the amount you need.

¼ tsp crumbled **saffron threads**

¾ cup warm **sodium-reduced chicken broth**

¼ tsp **salt**

1 lb (450 g) **boneless skinless chicken thighs,** cut in bite-size pieces

2 tbsp **olive oil**

Half each **onion** and **sweet red pepper,** diced

1 clove **garlic,** minced

1 tsp **tomato paste**

1 cup **arborio rice**

½ cup **dry white wine**

4 oz (115 g) **dry-cured chorizo sausage,** sliced

¼ tsp **smoked paprika** or sweet paprika

2 tbsp minced **fresh parsley**

Stir saffron into broth; let stand for 10 minutes. Meanwhile, sprinkle salt over chicken. In large skillet, heat half of the oil over medium-high heat; brown chicken. Transfer to plate.

Add remaining oil to pan; cook onion and red pepper over low heat until onion is translucent, about 10 minutes.

Stir in garlic and tomato paste; cook for 30 seconds. Stir in rice; cook, stirring, for 1 minute.

Add saffron broth, ¾ cup water, wine, chorizo and paprika. Return chicken to pan; bring to boil. Cover and cook over medium-low heat until rice is tender and no liquid remains, about 20 minutes. Stir in parsley. Let stand for 5 minutes.

Makes 4 servings. PER SERVING: about 536 cal, 33 g pro, 24 g total fat (7 g sat. fat), 44 g carb, 1 g fibre, 119 mg chol, 708 mg sodium, 516 mg potassium. % RDI: 3% calcium, 17% iron, 11% vit A, 50% vit C, 8% folate.

dinner with friends

Grilled Corn With Lime Chili Butter
Grilling corn gives it a smoky-sweet taste – perfect with the lime and chili–infused butter.

½ cup **butter,** softened

2 tbsp minced **fresh cilantro**

1 tsp **chili powder**

1 tsp grated **lime zest**

2 tbsp **lime juice**

12 cobs **corn,** husked

Stir together butter, cilantro, chili powder, lime zest and lime juice until smooth. Spoon onto plastic wrap; shape into log and wrap tightly. Or pack into small serving bowl, smoothing top. Refrigerate until firm. *(Make-ahead: Refrigerate for up to 2 weeks.)*

Meanwhile, place corn on greased grill over medium heat; grill, turning often, until softened and grill-marked, 15 to 20 minutes. Serve with lime chili butter.

Makes 12 servings. PER SERVING: about 199 cal, 4 g pro, 9 g total fat (5 g sat. fat), 31 g carb, 4 g fibre, 20 mg chol, 77 mg sodium, 309 mg potassium. % RDI: 1% calcium, 6% iron, 11% vit A, 15% vit C, 26% folate.

Coffee Caramel Sundaes
Even though this sweet finish is decidedly for grown-ups, it is yummy enough to bring out the kid in you.

¼ cup **strong brewed coffee,** cooled

1 tbsp **granulated sugar**

1 tbsp **dark rum** (optional)

8 **ladyfinger cookies**

4 cups **vanilla ice cream**

Chocolate shavings (optional),
  see Tip, below

COFFEE CARAMEL SAUCE:

¾ cup **strong brewed coffee,** cooled

½ cup **granulated sugar**

COFFEE CARAMEL SAUCE: In small saucepan, heat coffee until steaming; keep warm. In separate small saucepan, stir sugar with ¼ cup water over medium heat until dissolved. Boil over medium-high heat, brushing down side of pan with cold water but not stirring, until amber coloured, 5 to 6 minutes. Gradually pour in coffee, stirring constantly; boil vigorously until syrupy and reduced to ½ cup, 5 to 7 minutes. Let cool. *(Make-ahead: Refrigerate in airtight container for up to 3 days. Bring to room temperature to use.)*

In bowl, combine coffee, sugar, and rum (if using). Break ladyfingers into ½-inch (1 cm) pieces to make about 2⅓ cups; remove ⅓ cup and set aside for garnish. Add remaining ladyfingers to coffee mixture; toss to moisten. Set aside.

In another bowl, stir ice cream with wooden spoon until softened; fold in soaked ladyfingers. *(Make-ahead: Cover and freeze for up to 24 hours.)*

Spoon ¼ cup ice cream mixture into each of eight 1-cup glasses. Top each with about 1 tbsp coffee caramel sauce; top with remaining ice cream. Top with reserved ladyfingers, then remaining sauce. Garnish with chocolate shavings (if using).

Makes 8 servings. PER SERVING: about 211 cal, 3 g pro, 8 g total fat (5 g sat. fat), 34 g carb, 0 g fibre, 53 mg chol, 63 mg sodium. % RDI: 8% calcium, 2% iron, 9% vit A, 4% folate.

best **TIPS** ever

Shaved chocolate looks so elegant – and it couldn't be easier to make. Just shave the edge of a chocolate bar with a vegetable peeler. That's it! Make sure to use a spoon to pick up the shavings, because the heat of your hands can melt those delicate shards.

Strawberry Mascarpone Pizza
Toppings of mascarpone cheese and glazed strawberries create a sweet version of everyone's favourite food: pizza. To keep the crust crisp, top it right before serving.

1 pkg (397 g) **frozen puff pastry,** thawed

1 **egg yolk**

2 tbsp **granulated sugar**

½ cup **mascarpone cheese** or
   cream cheese

1 tbsp **milk**

2 tbsp **icing sugar**

¼ tsp **cinnamon**

¼ tsp **vanilla**

6 cups hulled **strawberries** (about 1½ lb/675 g)

¼ cup **strawberry jam** or strawberry jelly,
   melted and strained

Cut puff pastry in half to separate blocks; stack 1 on top of the other. On lightly floured surface, roll out pastry into 12-inch (30 cm) square. Trim corners to make circle. Transfer pastry to parchment paper–lined pizza pan; with fork, prick all over.

Whisk egg yolk with 1 tsp water; brush over pastry. Sprinkle with granulated sugar. Bake on bottom rack in 400°F (200°C) oven until puffed and golden, 15 to 18 minutes. Let cool on pan on rack. *(Make-ahead: Cover loosely with plastic wrap; store for up to 24 hours.)*

Meanwhile, in bowl, whisk mascarpone cheese with milk until smooth; whisk in icing sugar, cinnamon and vanilla. Cut strawberries in half.

Leaving ¼-inch (5 mm) border, spread cheese mixture over pastry. Arrange strawberries in concentric circles on top; brush berries with jam. Serve immediately.

Makes 8 servings. PER SERVING: about 415 cal, 5 g pro, 27 g total fat (7 g sat. fat), 40 g carb, 3 g fibre, 47 mg chol, 134 mg sodium. % RDI: 3% calcium, 13% iron, 2% vit A, 80% vit C, 20% folate.

grilling
get-together

Italian Stuffed Burgers

These savoury burgers are inspired by a traditional southern Italian recipe for stuffed meat loaf. The rich provolone and ham filling makes them a fun and interesting meal for entertaining.

Half pkg (300 g pkg) **frozen spinach,** thawed and drained (see Tip, page 44)

2 cloves **garlic,** minced

½ tsp each **salt** and **pepper**

1 **egg**

¼ cup **dried Italian bread crumbs**

¼ cup grated **Parmesan cheese**

1 tbsp chopped **fresh parsley**

1 lb (450 g) **lean ground veal** or lean ground beef

2 slices each **ham** and **provolone cheese**

In bowl, combine spinach and half each of the garlic, salt and pepper. Set aside.

In large bowl, beat egg; stir in bread crumbs, Parmesan cheese, parsley and remaining garlic, salt and pepper. Add veal; mix just until combined.

Place ham on cutting board; top each slice with 1 slice provolone cheese, then half of the spinach mixture. Roll up; cut in half. Shape veal mixture into four ¾-inch (2 cm) thick patties around ham roll-ups. *(Make-ahead: Layer between waxed paper in airtight container and refrigerate for up to 24 hours or freeze for up to 1 month. Thaw in refrigerator.)*

Place on greased grill over medium heat; close lid and grill, turning once, until instant-read thermometer inserted sideways into several reads 160°F (71°C), about 15 minutes.

Makes 4 servings. PER SERVING: about 293 cal, 33 g pro, 14 g total fat (7 g sat. fat), 7 g carb, 1 g fibre, 157 mg chol, 856 mg sodium. % RDI: 20% calcium, 14% iron, 25% vit A, 8% vit C, 20% folate.

Mixed Greens With Orange Chive Dressing

Instead of using packaged salad greens, make your own mix of mâche or baby spinach, frisée, Boston lettuce and arugula. Try it when local greens are at their peak.

3 **oranges**

3 tbsp **vegetable oil**

1 tbsp chopped **fresh chives**

½ tsp **Dijon mustard**

¼ tsp each **salt** and **pepper**

Half bulb **fennel,** cored

5 cups torn **mixed greens**

Cut off zest, pith and outer membranes of oranges; working over bowl to catch juice, cut between membranes and pulp to release fruit into bowl.

Drain off juice. Measure 2 tbsp into salad bowl; save remainder for another use (see Tip, below). Whisk oil, chives, mustard, salt and pepper into bowl; set aside.

With knife or mandoline, thinly slice fennel lengthwise; add to bowl along with greens and oranges; toss to coat.

Makes 6 servings. PER SERVING: about 97 cal, 2 g pro, 7 g total fat (1 g sat. fat), 9 g carb, 2 g fibre, 0 mg chol, 122 mg sodium, 308 mg potassium. % RDI: 5% calcium, 4% iron, 11% vit A, 58% vit C, 27% folate.

best **TIPS** ever

Citrus juice freezes well. Just spoon any leftovers into an ice-cube tray for easy-to-store single-portion cubes.

Mushrooms in Riesling

Riesling and mushrooms are an ideal match in this simple, flavourful appetizer. Serve with toothpicks for easy skewering.

3 tbsp **butter**

⅓ cup finely diced **shallots**

1 lb (450 g) **button mushrooms,**
   trimmed

1 tsp chopped **fresh thyme**
   (or ¼ tsp dried)

¼ tsp each **salt** and **pepper**

⅛ tsp **cayenne pepper**

½ cup **dry Riesling wine**

In large skillet, heat butter over medium heat; cook shallots for 3 minutes. Stir in mushrooms, thyme, salt, pepper and cayenne pepper; cook until deeply browned, about 5 minutes.

Pour in wine; bring to boil. Reduce heat and simmer, stirring, until no liquid remains, about 5 minutes. Serve warm.

Makes 8 to 10 servings. PER EACH OF 10 SERVINGS: about 51 cal, 2 g pro, 4 g total fat (2 g sat. fat), 3 g carb, 1 g fibre, 9 mg chol, 88 mg sodium. % RDI: 1% calcium, 1% iron, 4% vit A, 5% folate.

easy, elegant dinner

Blue Cheese & Peppercorn Tenderloins

Tender steak and creamy blue cheese? Yes, please! This is a gorgeous, romantic meal for two, but you can easily multiply the ingredients for more guests.

1 tbsp **black peppercorns**

1 clove **garlic,** minced

1 tbsp **Dijon mustard**

1 tbsp **olive oil**

2 **beef tenderloin grilling steaks**
   (about 6 oz/170 g each)

Pinch **salt**

2 tbsp crumbled **blue cheese**
   (see Tip, below)

Place peppercorns in resealable plastic bag. Using flat side of mallet or heavy saucepan, crush peppercorns; place in small bowl. Mix in garlic, mustard and oil. Spread around edge of each tenderloin.

In heavy skillet or on covered greased grill, cook steaks over high heat, turning once, until desired doneness, about 10 minutes for medium-rare. Sprinkle with salt.

Transfer to warmed platter; sprinkle with blue cheese. Tent with foil and let stand for 5 minutes before serving.

Makes 2 servings. PER SERVING: about 332 cal, 39 g pro, 17 g total fat (6 g sat. fat), 3 g carb, 1 g fibre, 86 mg chol, 295 mg sodium. % RDI: 7% calcium, 38% iron, 2% vit A, 2% vit C, 5% folate.

best **TIPS** ever

Danish blue cheese is reasonably priced, but if you're splurging on tenderloin, try a splashier blue, such as Bleu Bénédictin or Ermite from here in Canada. Or try a creamy French Roquefort. You don't need a large quantity, and it's worth the price.

Green Goddess Dressing

If you like, boost the tarragon flavour by using tarragon vinegar instead of plain.

1 cup **fresh parsley leaves**

½ cup each **light sour cream** and **light mayonnaise**

1 **green onion,** chopped

2 tbsp **vinegar**

1 tbsp **dried tarragon**
   (or 3 tbsp chopped fresh tarragon)

¼ tsp each **salt** and **pepper**

In food processor, purée together parsley, sour cream, mayonnaise, green onion, vinegar, tarragon, salt and pepper. *(Make-ahead: Refrigerate in airtight container for up to 1 week.)*

Makes 1 cup. PER 1 TBSP: about 35 cal, 1 g pro, 3 g total fat (1 g sat. fat), 2 g carb, trace fibre, 4 mg chol, 95 mg sodium, 49 mg potassium. % RDI: 2% calcium, 2% iron, 4% vit A, 8% vit C, 3% folate.

Balsamic-Glazed Figs

Sweetening and boiling down balsamic vinegar transforms it into a sophisticated syrup that's also nice over strawberries.

½ cup **balsamic vinegar**

3 tbsp packed **brown sugar**

6 **fresh figs**

¾ cup **mascarpone cheese**

In small saucepan, bring vinegar and brown sugar to boil over medium-high heat; reduce heat and simmer until reduced to scant ¼ cup, about 10 minutes. Keep warm. *(Make-ahead: Let cool. Store in airtight container for up to 1 month. Reheat to continue.)*

Cut figs in half. Brush with one-quarter of the balsamic glaze. Place on greased grill over medium-low heat; close lid and grill, turning once, until softened, about 6 minutes.

Arrange 2 halves on each plate; add spoonful of mascarpone cheese. Drizzle with remaining glaze.

Makes 6 servings. PER SERVING: about 214 cal, 2 g pro, 14 g total fat (9 g sat. fat), 23 g carb, 2 g fibre, 42 mg chol, 11 mg sodium. % RDI: 4% calcium, 2% iron, 1% vit A, 2% vit C, 1% folate.

Honey Roast Chicken With Onions & Figs Crispy on the outside and juicy on the inside, this golden chicken is the ideal Sunday dinner.

2 tbsp **vegetable oil**

2 tsp **liquid honey**

¼ tsp each **salt** and **pepper**

1 **whole chicken** (about 3½ lb/1.5 kg)

1 small **onion**

4 cloves **garlic**

Half **lemon**

2 sprigs **fresh thyme**

4 cups **pearl onions** (about two 284 g pkg), peeled

2 cups **dried whole Calimyrna figs**

1 tbsp **all-purpose flour**

½ cup **white wine**

1 cup **chicken broth**

Whisk together 1 tbsp of the oil, 1 tsp of the honey, salt and pepper; set aside.

Remove giblets and neck from chicken. Rinse chicken inside and out; pat dry. Insert onion, garlic, lemon and thyme into cavity. Tie legs together with kitchen string; tuck wings under back. Place, breast side up, on greased rack in roasting pan. Toss pearl onions with remaining oil and add to pan.

Roast in 375°F (190°C) oven for 30 minutes; brush with honey mixture. Roast until instant-read thermometer inserted into thickest part of breast reads 170°F (77°C) and juices run clear when chicken is pierced, about 30 minutes. Set pearl onions aside. Transfer chicken to warmed platter and tent with foil; let stand for 20 minutes before carving. Discard onion, garlic, lemon and thyme from cavity.

Meanwhile, remove hard stems from figs; set figs aside.

Skim fat from pan juices. Whisk in flour; cook, whisking, for 1 minute. Add wine; cook, whisking, until most of the liquid is evaporated, about 1 minute. Add broth, scraping up any browned bits from bottom of pan; simmer, whisking, until smooth, slightly thickened and glossy. Add pearl onions, figs and remaining honey to pan; simmer, stirring, until figs are hot, about 2 minutes. Using slotted spoon, remove onions and figs; arrange around chicken on platter. Strain gravy into serving dish; serve with chicken.

Makes 4 to 6 servings. PER EACH OF 6 SERVINGS: about 449 cal, 25 g pro, 17 g total fat (4 g sat. fat), 51 g carb, 9 g fibre, 81 mg chol, 304 mg sodium. % RDI: 11% calcium, 19% iron, 5% vit A, 17% vit C, 7% folate.

fancy roast
chicken dinner

Roasted Beet
& Arugula Salad With Walnut Dressing Classic and
colourful, this is a striking salad both in looks and flavour.

1½ lb (675 g) **beets** (6 to 8)

4 cloves **garlic,** sliced

1 sprig **fresh rosemary** (or 1 tsp dried)

3 tbsp **extra-virgin olive oil**

½ tsp each **salt** and **pepper**

8 cups **arugula**

1 cup toasted **walnuts,**
    coarsely chopped

WALNUT VINAIGRETTE:

⅓ cup **walnut oil** (see Tip, below)
    or extra-virgin olive oil

1 small **shallot** (or half green onion),
    minced

3 tbsp **cider vinegar**

½ tsp **dry mustard**

¼ tsp each **salt** and **pepper**

Pinch **granulated sugar**

Cut off beet greens, leaving 1-inch (2.5 cm) tails; save greens for another use. Place beets on 20-inch (50 cm) piece of foil. Sprinkle with garlic, rosemary, oil, salt and pepper; fold and seal edges to form packet. Roast on baking sheet in 400°F (200°C) oven until fork-tender, about 1½ hours. Let cool enough to handle.

Peel and trim beets; cut into 1-inch (2.5 cm) thick wedges. *(Make-ahead: Cover and refrigerate for up to 24 hours. Serve at room temperature.)*

WALNUT VINAIGRETTE: In large bowl, whisk together oil, shallot, vinegar, mustard, salt, pepper and sugar. Transfer 2 tbsp to separate bowl; add beets and toss to coat.

Add arugula to remaining vinaigrette; toss to coat. Divide among plates; top with beets. Sprinkle with walnuts.

Makes 8 servings. PER SERVING: about 254 cal, 3 g pro, 24 g total fat (2 g sat. fat), 10 g carb, 2 g fibre, 0 mg chol, 266 mg sodium. % RDI: 3% calcium, 8% iron, 1% vit A, 5% vit C, 30% folate.

best
TIPS
ever

Nut oils can go rancid quickly at room temperature, so keep them in the fridge or freezer. Buy small quantities and use them often.

Chive & Parsley Mashed Potatoes

Cream and butter are the keys to the silky texture of these make-ahead potatoes.

8 cups cubed peeled **potatoes** (3 lb/1.35 kg)

¼ cup **whipping cream (35%)**

2 tbsp each minced **fresh chives** and
   fresh parsley

1 tbsp **butter**

½ tsp **salt**

¼ tsp **pepper**

In large pot of boiling salted water, cover and cook potatoes until tender, about 10 minutes. Drain and return to pot over low heat to dry for 30 seconds. Press through food mill or potato ricer, or mash. Return to pot.

In small saucepan, heat together cream, chives, parsley, butter, salt and pepper until steaming; pour over potatoes and mash together. Scrape into serving bowl. *(Make-ahead: Let cool for 30 minutes. Refrigerate, uncovered, until cold. Cover and refrigerate for up to 24 hours. Reheat in microwaveable bowl at high, about 5 minutes.)*

Makes 8 servings. PER SERVING: about 154 cal, 3 g pro, 4 g total fat (3 g sat. fat), 27 g carb, 2 g fibre, 13 mg chol, 482 mg sodium. % RDI: 2% calcium, 4% iron, 4% vit A, 18% vit C, 6% folate.

Cinnamon Mousse

Serve these light, creamy cinnamon desserts, called *bavarois* in French, topped with fresh raspberries or orange segments.

2 tsp **unflavoured gelatin**

1 cup **milk**

¾ tsp **cinnamon**

2 **egg yolks**

3 tbsp **granulated sugar**

½ tsp **vanilla**

⅔ cup **whipping cream (35%)**

GARNISH:

¼ tsp **cinnamon**

Sprinkle gelatin over 2 tbsp water; let stand for 5 minutes to soften. Meanwhile, in small heavy saucepan, heat milk and cinnamon over medium heat until bubbles form around edge.

In bowl, whisk egg yolks with sugar; slowly whisk in hot milk. Return to saucepan and cook, stirring, over medium-low heat until mixture is thick enough to coat back of spoon, about 10 minutes. Remove from heat. Add softened gelatin; stir until dissolved. Add vanilla. Pour into large bowl. Place plastic wrap directly on surface; refrigerate, stirring twice, until consistency of egg whites, about 1 hour.

Whip cream; fold one-quarter into gelatin mixture. Fold in remaining whipped cream. Pour into 4 greased 6-oz (175 mL) fluted moulds or ramekins. Cover and refrigerate until firm, about 6 hours. *(Make-ahead: Refrigerate for up to 2 days.)*

GARNISH: One at a time, run knife around edge of mould, or warm mould for a few seconds in hot water. Invert chilled serving plate onto mould; invert to unmould mousse. Using fine-mesh sieve, dust cinnamon over mousse and plates.

Makes 4 servings. PER SERVING: about 234 cal, 6 g pro, 18 g total fat (10 g sat. fat), 14 g carb, trace fibre, 157 mg chol, 52 mg sodium. % RDI: 11% calcium, 4% iron, 23% vit A, 2% vit C, 8% folate.

Greek Phyllo-Wrapped Chicken (opposite)
and Green Beans Amandine (page 71)

Greek Phyllo-Wrapped Chicken

All over Greece, delicate phyllo pastry encloses savoury and sweet ingredients in pies called *pita*. Here, we incorporate those traditional flavours into an easy make-ahead dish that's family-friendly yet elegant enough for company.

1 cup crumbled **feta cheese**

2 **egg yolks**

1 clove **garlic,** minced

½ cup chopped **green onions**

⅓ cup each chopped **fresh parsley** and **fresh mint**

¼ tsp **pepper**

4 **boneless skinless chicken breasts**

8 sheets **phyllo pastry**

⅓ cup **butter,** melted

Lemon wedges

In bowl, mash together feta cheese, egg yolks and garlic. Mix in green onions, parsley, mint and pepper.

With sharp knife held horizontally and starting at rounded side of breast, cut chicken in half almost but not all the way through; open like book. Spread feta mixture evenly over 1 half of each; fold uncovered half over filling to enclose.

Place 1 sheet of phyllo on work surface, keeping remainder covered with damp towel to prevent drying out. Brush lightly with some of the butter; top with second sheet and brush lightly with butter. Centre 1 chicken breast on phyllo about 2 inches (5 cm) from 1 short edge; fold long sides over chicken and roll up. Repeat to make 4 pieces total. Place in lightly greased baking dish; brush with remaining butter. *(Make-ahead: Cover and refrigerate for up to 8 hours.)*

Bake in 350°F (180°C) oven until crisp and golden, about 45 minutes. Serve with lemon wedges.

Makes 4 servings. PER SERVING: about 553 cal, 40 g pro, 30 g total fat (16 g sat. fat), 29 g carb, 2 g fibre, 248 mg chol, 822 mg sodium. % RDI: 19% calcium, 24% iron, 28% vit A, 10% vit C, 23% folate.

easy entertaining menu

Warm Garlic Bean Crostini

White beans laced with garlic are so tasty atop crusty crostini. Partially crushing the beans gives this spread a chunkier, more substantial texture than regular bean dip.

1 **baguette** (24 inches/60 cm)

2 tbsp **extra-virgin olive oil**

3 cloves **garlic,** minced

½ tsp crumbled **dried sage**

¼ tsp **pepper**

1 can (19 oz/540 mL) **white kidney beans,**
   drained and rinsed

1 tsp grated **lemon zest** (see Tip, below)

1 tbsp **lemon juice**

Small fresh sage leaves or
   fresh parsley leaves (optional)

Cut baguette diagonally into 24 slices. Broil on baking sheet, turning once, until golden on both sides, 1 minute. Set aside.

In nonstick skillet, heat oil over medium heat; cook garlic, sage and pepper, stirring, until garlic is golden, 1 minute.

Meanwhile, in bowl, mash one-third of the kidney beans. Add mashed and whole beans, lemon zest and lemon juice to skillet; cook until hot, about 3 minutes. Spoon heaping 1 tbsp onto each crostini. Garnish with sage (if using).

Makes 24 pieces. PER PIECE: about 66 cal, 2 g pro, 2 g total fat (trace sat. fat), 10 g carb, 2 g fibre, 0 mg chol, 124 mg sodium. % RDI: 1% calcium, 4% iron, 2% vit C, 7% folate.

best **TIPS** ever

Lemon, or other citrus, zest gives a fresh burst of sunny flavour to both sweet and savoury dishes. The key is to grate gently so that none of the bitter white pith is attached to the zest. A handheld rasp is the simplest tool to use, and it cleans up much more easily than an old-fashioned box grater.

Green Beans Amandine

This old-school side is a perennial fave. The crunchy almonds are the perfect complement to the buttery beans.

⅔ cup **sliced almonds**

2 tbsp **butter**

¼ tsp **salt**

1 lb (450 g) **green beans,** trimmed

In dry skillet over medium-high heat, toast almonds just until golden, about 4 minutes. Remove and set aside.

Add ¾ cup water, butter and salt to skillet; bring to boil. Add beans; reduce heat, cover and simmer until bright green, about 3 minutes.

Uncover and simmer, turning beans often, until tender and no liquid remains, about 8 minutes. Toss with almonds.

Makes 4 to 6 servings. PER EACH OF 6 SERVINGS: about 116 cal, 4 g pro, 9 g total fat (3 g sat. fat), 7 g carb, 3 g fibre, 10 mg chol, 126 mg sodium, 161 mg potassium. % RDI: 5% calcium, 6% iron, 8% vit A, 10% vit C, 10% folate.

Lemon Mint Tarts

Frozen tart shells are so convenient for this recipe, but you can use your favourite pastry to make your own if you have time.

¾ cup **granulated sugar**

2 tbsp **butter,** softened

1 tbsp grated **lemon zest**

¼ cup **lemon juice**

2 **eggs,** beaten

1 tsp **dried mint** (or 2 tsp finely chopped fresh mint)

12 **frozen tart shells**

In bowl, beat sugar with butter; beat in lemon zest, lemon juice, eggs and mint. Place tart shells on rimmed baking sheet; pour in lemon filling.

Bake in 375°F (190°C) oven until filling is set, about 20 minutes. Let cool on rack. *(Make-ahead: Refrigerate in airtight container for up to 2 days.)*

Makes 12 tarts. PER TART: about 178 cal, 2 g pro, 9 g total fat (3 g sat. fat), 22 g carb, trace fibre, 41 mg chol, 151 mg sodium. % RDI: 1% calcium, 4% iron, 4% vit A, 5% vit C, 3% folate.

From top: Grilled Shrimp With Citrus Aïoli (page 75),
Vietnamese Lettuce Cups (page 74)
and Pear & Brie Triangles (opposite)

Pear & Brie Triangles
Juicy pear, creamy cheese and flaky puff pastry bites look fancy but are truly easy and quick to make. You can also try the triangles with apple instead of pear.

1 pkg (397 g) **frozen puff pastry,** thawed

8 oz (225 g) **Brie cheese**

1 **pear**

2 tbsp **lemon juice**

1 tbsp **vegetable oil**

1 tsp chopped **fresh thyme**

On lightly floured surface, roll out half of the pastry into 12- x 8-inch (30 x 20 cm) rectangle; cut in half lengthwise. Cut each half crosswise into quarters; cut each piece in half diagonally to make 16 triangles total.

Place pastry triangles on parchment paper–lined baking sheet; prick all over with fork. Bake in 375°F (190°C) oven until golden and puffed, about 10 minutes. Let cool on rack. Repeat with remaining pastry. *(Make-ahead: Store in airtight container for up to 24 hours.)*

Meanwhile, cut Brie cheese into 32 thin slices. Quarter pear lengthwise, removing core; cut each quarter lengthwise into 8 thin strips. Place 1 piece of cheese on each pastry triangle; top with pear strip.

Stir together lemon juice, oil and thyme; brush over pear and cheese. Bake until cheese starts to melt, about 5 minutes.

Makes 32 pieces. PER PIECE: about 101 cal, 2 g pro, 7 g total fat (2 g sat. fat), 7 g carb, trace fibre, 7 mg chol, 77 mg sodium. % RDI: 1% calcium, 3% iron, 1% vit A, 5% folate.

girls' night in

Vietnamese Lettuce Cups

This sautéed pork appetizer is colourful and tasty – and you can make it ahead, which means less last-minute prep before the party. The lettuce cups make it fun to eat.

Half small **ripe mango**

4 heads **Sweet Gem lettuce** or
  1 head Bibb lettuce

½ cup finely diced **sweet red pepper**

FILLING:

1 tbsp **vegetable oil**

12 oz (340 g) **lean ground pork**

½ cup minced **red onion**

2 cloves **garlic,** minced

1 tbsp minced **fresh ginger**

½ tsp **cinnamon**

¼ tsp **hot pepper flakes**

Pinch **ground cloves** (see Tip, below)

1 tbsp **fish sauce**

1 tbsp **lime juice**

2 tsp **soy sauce**

1 tsp **cornstarch**

2 tbsp minced **fresh cilantro**

FILLING: In skillet, heat oil over medium heat; cook pork, breaking up with spoon, until no longer pink, 5 minutes. Add onion, garlic, ginger, cinnamon, hot pepper flakes and cloves; fry until onion is softened, 3 minutes. Stir in fish sauce; cover and simmer over medium-low heat for 3 minutes. Stir together lime juice, soy sauce and cornstarch until smooth; stir into pork mixture and cook until slightly thickened, 2 minutes. Let cool. *(Make-ahead: Refrigerate in airtight container for up to 2 days.)* Stir in cilantro.

Peel and cut mango into ¼-inch (5 mm) thick slices; cut into ¼-inch (5 mm) thick sticks. Separate lettuce to make twenty-four 3-inch (8 cm) cups, trimming any large leaves if necessary. *(Make-ahead: Cover and refrigerate separately for up to 4 hours.)*

Mound 1 tbsp of the filling in each lettuce cup. Garnish with mango and red pepper.

Makes 24 pieces. PER PIECE: about 43 cal, 3 g pro, 3 g total fat (1 g sat. fat), 2 g carb, trace fibre, 8 mg chol, 94 mg sodium. % RDI: 1% calcium, 1% iron, 4% vit A, 13% vit C, 4% folate.

best **TIPS** ever

A spice grinder is a great investment. Already-ground spices from the supermarket can become stale very quickly, but whole spices will hang on to their flavours and aromas longer. With a spice grinder in the kitchen, you can grind just the amount you need for a recipe – like the pinch of ground cloves for these lettuce cups – and get the brightest flavour. You also won't have as many spice jars filling up the cupboards!

Grilled Shrimp With Citrus Aïoli

Use the mix of citrus fruit suggested or substitute the total amount (1½ tsp grated zest and 1 tbsp juice) of one favourite in the aïoli.

12 oz (340 g) **raw jumbo shrimp,** peeled and deveined

2 tsp **extra-virgin olive oil**

¼ tsp **ground cumin**

Pinch each **cayenne pepper** and **salt**

CITRUS AÏOLI:

⅓ cup **light mayonnaise**

½ tsp each grated **orange, lemon** and **lime zest**

1 tsp each **orange, lemon** and **lime juice**

1 small clove **garlic,** minced

Pinch **pepper**

CITRUS AÏOLI: Whisk together mayonnaise; orange, lemon and lime zests and juices; garlic; and pepper. *(Make-ahead: Refrigerate in airtight container for up to 2 days.)*

Stir together shrimp, oil, cumin, cayenne pepper and salt. Place shrimp on greased grill over medium-high heat; close lid and grill, turning once, until shrimp are pink and opaque, about 4 minutes. Transfer to plate; refrigerate until cold. *(Make-ahead: Refrigerate in airtight container for up to 24 hours.)*

Skewer shrimp with toothpicks; serve with citrus aïoli.

Makes 4 servings. PER SERVING: about 152 cal, 13 g pro, 9 g total fat (1 g sat. fat), 3 g carb, trace fibre, 103 mg chol, 241 mg sodium. % RDI: 3% calcium, 12% iron, 3% vit A, 7% vit C, 2% folate.

Candy Apple Martini

A signature cocktail is a terrific way to start your girls' night in. This ruby red martini tastes just like a candy apple – it's dangerously delicious!

Ice cubes

1 oz (2 tbsp) **vodka**

1 oz (2 tbsp) **apple schnapps**

1 oz (2 tbsp) **pomegranate juice**

½ oz (1 tbsp) **butterscotch schnapps**

Thin wheel **red-skinned apple**

Fill cocktail shaker with ice. Add vodka, apple schnapps, pomegranate juice and butterscotch schnapps; shake vigorously to blend and chill. Strain into martini glass; float apple wheel on top.

Makes 1 serving. PER SERVING: about 191 cal, 0 g pro, 0 g total fat (0 g sat. fat), 19 g carb, trace fibre, 0 mg chol, 3 mg sodium, 10 mg potassium. % RDI: 2% vit C.

Raspberry Chipotle Wings

Hot and richly fruity, this sauce also makes a great glaze for salmon, sausages or meatballs. Or pour over goat cheese or warmed Brie and serve with crackers.

3 lb (1.35 kg) **chicken wings**

2 tbsp **vegetable oil**

1 **onion,** chopped

2 cups **fresh raspberries** or thawed frozen unsweetened raspberries

2 tbsp **raspberry vinegar** or red wine vinegar

2 tbsp **fancy molasses**

1 tbsp **liquid honey**

1 tbsp chopped **canned chipotle in adobo sauce**

1 tsp each **salt** and **pepper**

Remove tips from chicken wings and reserve for stock if desired; separate wings at joint.

In small saucepan, heat oil over medium heat; fry onion, stirring occasionally, until softened, about 5 minutes.

Add raspberries, vinegar, molasses, honey, chipotle and half each of the salt and pepper; bring to boil. Reduce heat and simmer, stirring often, until reduced by half, about 12 minutes. Let cool slightly.

Scrape into blender; purée. Pressing on solids, strain through fine-mesh sieve into large bowl. Set aside. *(Make-ahead: Refrigerate in airtight container for up to 2 days.)*

Toss wings with remaining salt and pepper. Place on greased grill rack or in grill basket over medium heat; close lid and grill, turning occasionally, until crisp and juices run clear when chicken is pierced, about 30 minutes. (To roast wings, arrange wings on rack on foil-lined rimmed baking sheet; roast in 400°F/200°C oven, turning once, for 45 minutes.)

Add to raspberry mixture in bowl; toss to coat. Return to grill or oven; grill or roast, covered and turning once, for 4 minutes. Serve with remaining sauce for dipping.

Makes 6 servings. PER SERVING: about 315 cal, 21 g pro, 20 g total fat (4 g sat. fat), 13 g carb, 0 g fibre, 63 mg chol, 469 mg sodium. % RDI: 4% calcium, 12% iron, 6% vit A, 13% vit C, 5% folate.

wing night

Parmesan Mustard Wings

These flavourful wings are roasted (not fried), so they're crispy but not greasy. Parmesan cheese is fairly mild, but Romano cheese will give the wings a sharper taste.

2½ lb (1.125 kg) **chicken wings** (about 17)

¼ cup **Dijon mustard**

2 tbsp **lemon juice**

¼ tsp **cayenne pepper**

¼ tsp **salt**

½ cup **dried bread crumbs**

¼ cup grated **Parmesan cheese** or Romano cheese

2 tbsp minced **fresh parsley**

Remove tips from chicken wings and reserve for stock if desired; separate wings at joint. Trim off excess skin. Place wings in large bowl.

Add Dijon mustard, lemon juice, cayenne pepper and salt; toss to coat well.

In shallow dish, combine bread crumbs, Parmesan cheese and parsley; press wings into mixture to coat all over. Arrange on rack on foil-lined rimmed baking sheet. *(Make-ahead: Cover and refrigerate for up to 4 hours.)*

Roast in 400°F (200°C) oven, turning once, until crisp and juices run clear when wings are pierced, about 40 minutes.

Makes 34 pieces. PER PIECE: about 51 cal, 4 g pro, 3 g total fat (1 g sat. fat), 1 g carb, 0 g fibre, 11 mg chol, 78 mg sodium. % RDI: 2% calcium, 2% iron, 1% vit A.

Creamy Cucumber Salad

Salting and draining the cucumber keeps it from making this lovely dressing watery.

3 cups thinly sliced peeled
   English cucumber

1 tsp **salt**

½ cup thinly sliced **red onion**

¼ cup **light sour cream** or
   regular sour cream 1 tbsp chopped **fresh dill** (or
   1 tsp dried dillweed)

1 tbsp **white wine vinegar**

1 tsp **granulated sugar**

In colander, sprinkle cucumber with salt; let drain for 30 minutes. Pat dry.

Meanwhile, soak onion in cold water for 15 minutes; drain and pat dry.

In bowl, whisk together sour cream, dill, vinegar and sugar. Add cucumber and onion; toss to coat.

Makes 4 servings. PER SERVING: about 38 cal, 2 g pro, 1 g total fat (1 g sat. fat), 6 g carb, 1 g fibre, 2 mg chol, 302 mg sodium. % RDI: 4% calcium, 1% iron, 1% vit A, 7% vit C, 7% folate.

Stuffed Chive Potatoes

Fluffy insides and crispy tops make these chive-studded baked potatoes hard to resist.

4 **baking potatoes** (see Tips, below)

½ cup **light sour cream**

¼ cup minced **fresh chives** (see Tips, below)

2 tbsp **butter**

½ tsp each **salt** and **pepper**

Using fork, prick each potato several times. Bake in 400°F (200°C) oven until tender, about 1 hour.

Cut thin slice lengthwise off each potato. Leaving ½-inch (1 cm) thick walls, scoop flesh into bowl. Mash in sour cream, chives, butter and half each of salt and pepper.

Sprinkle shells with remaining salt and pepper; spoon in potato mixture, mounding slightly. Place on rimmed baking sheet. (Make-ahead: Cover and refrigerate for up to 24 hours. Uncover and bake in 375°F/190°C oven until hot, about 20 minutes.)

Broil until tops are golden, about 3 minutes.

Makes 4 servings. PER SERVING: about 236 cal, 4 g pro, 10 g total fat (6 g sat. fat), 34 g carb, 3 g fibre, 29 mg chol, 368 mg sodium. % RDI: 4% calcium, 14% iron, 10% vit A, 30% vit C, 9% folate.

best **TIPS** ever

• Long oval baking potatoes, such as russet, offer the fluffiest results for this recipe. Their floury texture also makes them ideal for frying and mashing. Round white or red potatoes have a waxy texture that's better suited to boiling. Yellow-fleshed potatoes are all-purpose superstars; they can be used in most recipes with great results.

• If you're out of fresh chives, green onions are a slightly stronger alternative.

From top: Tagine of Beef With Prunes (opposite) and Chickpea, Feta & Raisin Couscous (page 83)

Tagine of Beef With Prunes

Tagine is the name of both the pan and the stew that's cooked in it. But this Moroccan staple is just as delicious when it's made in a regular Dutch oven or large saucepan.

¼ cup **all-purpose flour**

½ tsp **salt**

1½ lb (675 g) **stewing beef cubes,** trimmed and cut in bite-size pieces

2 tbsp **olive oil** or vegetable oil

4 **onions,** quartered

4 cloves **garlic,** sliced

3 large **carrots,** chopped

1 rib **celery,** sliced

2 tsp **ground cumin**

1 tsp **ground coriander**

1 tsp **sweet paprika**

¼ tsp **cinnamon**

¼ tsp **cayenne pepper**

2½ cups **beef broth**

¼ cup **tomato paste**

1 tbsp **red wine vinegar**

1 **orange**

2 cups **pitted prunes**

¼ cup chopped **fresh parsley**

¼ cup sliced **green onions**

In shallow dish, stir flour with salt; add beef, turning to coat all over. In Dutch oven or large heavy saucepan, heat half of the oil over medium-high heat; brown beef, in batches, about 10 minutes. Transfer to plate.

Add remaining oil to pan; reduce heat to medium. Add onions, garlic, carrots, celery, cumin, coriander, paprika, cinnamon and cayenne pepper; cook, stirring often, until vegetables are softened, about 8 minutes.

Return beef and any accumulated juices to pan; stir in broth, tomato paste and vinegar. Cut 2 long strips of orange zest; add to pan. Squeeze ⅓ cup juice from orange; add to pan. Bring to boil; reduce heat, cover and simmer, stirring occasionally, for 1½ hours.

Add prunes; simmer until beef is tender, uncovering if necessary to thicken sauce, about 30 minutes. Serve sprinkled with parsley and green onions.

Makes 6 servings. PER SERVING: about 482 cal, 27 g pro, 18 g total fat (6 g sat. fat), 58 g carb, 8 g fibre, 67 mg chol, 864 mg sodium, 1,189 mg potassium. % RDI: 9% calcium, 35% iron, 90% vit A, 37% vit C, 18% folate.

moroccan-inspired feast

Garlic Flatbread

Flatbreads are common across the globe, and they're wonderful for dunking in delicious sauces, stews and dips alike. This one has just the right amount of garlic to give it a little extra *oomph*.

Pinch **granulated sugar**

¾ cup **warm water**

1 tsp **active dry yeast** or
   quick-rising (instant) dry yeast

3 tbsp **extra-virgin olive oil**

1¾ cups **all-purpose flour**

¾ tsp **salt**

1 clove **garlic,** minced

¼ tsp **dried mint** or
   dried oregano

In large bowl, dissolve sugar in warm water. Sprinkle in yeast; let stand until frothy, about 10 minutes. Whisk in 2 tbsp of the oil. Stir in flour, about ¼ cup at a time, and salt to form sticky dough.

Turn out onto lightly floured surface; knead until smooth, about 5 minutes. Place in greased bowl, turning to grease all over; cover and let rise in warm draft-free place until doubled in bulk, about 1½ hours.

Turn out dough onto lightly floured surface; press fingertips into dough to create dimples. Gently stretch into 15- x 6-inch (38 x 15 cm) rectangle. Transfer to greased rimless baking sheet. Cover and let rise in warm draft-free place until nearly doubled in bulk, about 45 minutes.

Bake in 400°F (200°C) oven for 13 minutes. Meanwhile, stir together remaining oil, garlic and mint; brush over flatbread. Bake until light golden around edges, about 5 minutes.

Makes 4 to 6 servings. PER EACH OF 6 SERVINGS: about 195 cal, 4 g pro, 7 g total fat (1 g sat. fat), 28 g carb, 1 g fibre, 0 mg chol, 289 mg sodium. % RDI: 1% calcium, 14% iron, 41% folate.

best
TIPS
ever

- Active dry yeast and quick-rising (dry) yeast are normally not interchangeable. This flatbread, however, doesn't require a big rise, so either will work fine.

- Keep yeast packages in the fridge to preserve their freshness. Check the use-by date and buy new if you suspect yours is inactive. To proof yeast, or check that it's still working, in bowl, mix ¼ tsp granulated sugar with 1 cup warm water; sprinkle ½ tsp yeast over top and let stand for 10 minutes. If the mixture turns frothy, the yeast is active and ready for baking.

Chickpea, Feta & Raisin Couscous
For a restaurant-style presentation, pack this couscous into 3½- x 1½-inch (175 mL) greased ramekins, custard cups or timbale moulds, then invert onto plates.

1 tbsp **vegetable oil**

1 **onion,** chopped

2 cloves **garlic,** minced

1 cup drained rinsed **canned chickpeas**

2 tbsp **raisins** or dried currants

½ tsp **ground cumin**

¼ tsp each **salt** and **pepper**

1½ cups **vegetable broth**

1 cup **whole wheat couscous** or regular couscous

½ cup crumbled **feta cheese**

2 tbsp chopped **fresh parsley**

In saucepan, heat oil over medium heat; cook onion, garlic, chickpeas, raisins, cumin, salt and pepper, stirring often, until onion is softened, about 4 minutes.

Add broth; bring to boil. Stir in couscous; remove from heat. Cover and let stand for 5 minutes.

Add feta cheese and parsley; fluff with fork.

Makes 4 servings. PER SERVING: about 345 cal, 13 g pro, 9 g total fat (3 g sat. fat), 58 g carb, 9 g fibre, 19 mg chol, 764 mg sodium, 270 mg potassium. % RDI: 13% calcium, 19% iron, 5% vit A, 10% vit C, 21% folate.

Tequila Swizzles

A pitcher of this refreshing cocktail is the perfect start to a Mexican-inspired menu. Serve in tall glasses garnished with thin slices of lime, and add straws or swizzle sticks for stirring.

1 cup **lime juice** (6 to 8 limes)
½ cup **granulated sugar**
1½ cups **white (silver) tequila**
Ice cubes
2½ cups **soda water**
6 dashes **Angostura bitters** (approx)
Lime wheels or wedges

In glass measure, combine lime juice with sugar. Microwave at high for 20 seconds; stir until sugar is dissolved. Stir in tequila. *(Make-ahead: Cover and refrigerate for up to 4 hours.)*

Fill pitcher halfway with ice cubes. Add tequila mixture, soda water and bitters; stir to combine. Add more bitters if desired. Garnish with lime wheels.

Makes 8 servings. PER SERVING: about 153 cal, trace pro, 0 g total fat (0 g sat. fat), 15 g carb, trace fibre, 0 mg chol, 17 mg sodium. % RDI: 1% calcium, 1% iron, 15% vit C, 1% folate.

fajita
fiesta

Guacamole Shrimp on Cornmeal Pancakes

Colourful bites of shrimp, guacamole and pancake are an irresistible starter. Want to make them even more decadent? Add a tiny dollop of Mexican *crema* or sour cream.

24 **cooked large shrimp**
   (about 10 oz/280 g total)
24 leaves **fresh cilantro**

GUACAMOLE:

1 clove **garlic,** minced
1 tbsp minced **jalapeño pepper**
1 tbsp **lime juice** or lemon juice
Pinch each **salt** and **pepper**
1 small **ripe avocado**

CORNMEAL PANCAKES:

½ cup **all-purpose flour**
2 tbsp **cornmeal**
1 tsp each **granulated sugar** and
   baking powder
¼ tsp **salt**
1 **egg yolk**
⅔ cup **milk**
4 tsp **vegetable oil**

CORNMEAL PANCAKES: In bowl, whisk together flour, cornmeal, sugar, baking powder and salt. Whisk together egg yolk, milk and oil; stir into dry ingredients just until a few lumps remain.

Using scant 1 tbsp batter for each pancake (see Tip, below) and brushing skillet with oil as necessary, cook pancakes over medium heat until bottoms are golden and bubbles break on tops, about 1 minute. Turn and cook until bottoms are golden, about 1 minute. *(Make-ahead: Let cool. Layer between waxed paper in airtight container and refrigerate for up to 24 hours or freeze for up to 2 weeks. Reheat in 350°F/180°C oven until hot, about 5 minutes if refrigerated; 7 minutes if frozen.)*

GUACAMOLE: In bowl, combine garlic, jalapeño pepper, lime juice, salt and pepper. Peel, pit and dice avocado; add to bowl and mash until slightly chunky. *(Make-ahead: Add pit to guacamole; cover and refrigerate for up to 4 hours.)*

Spoon about 1 tsp guacamole onto each pancake; top each with 1 shrimp and 1 cilantro leaf.

Makes 24 pieces. PER PIECE: about 48 cal, 3 g pro, 2 g total fat (trace sat. fat), 4 g carb, trace fibre, 32 mg chol, 66 mg sodium. % RDI: 2% calcium, 4% iron, 2% vit A, 3% vit C, 5% folate.

best **TIPS** ever

For appetizer pancakes like these, it's nice to have a uniform size. Use a tablespoon measure to drop the batter into the pan – it's just as easy but more accurate than eyeballing it.

Grilled Chicken Fajitas

Using skinless chicken is a healthy and delicious way to cut back on fat in this tasty main.

1 lb (450 g) **boneless skinless chicken breasts**

Half each **sweet green pepper** and **sweet red pepper,** halved lengthwise

4 **large whole wheat tortillas**

2 cups shredded **lettuce**

1 cup shredded **part-skim mozzarella cheese** or light provolone cheese

MARINADE:

2 tbsp **vegetable oil**

1 tsp **chili powder**

½ tsp **smoked paprika** or sweet paprika

¼ tsp **ground cumin**

¼ tsp each **salt** and **pepper**

MARINADE: Stir together oil, chili powder, paprika, cumin, salt and pepper; brush over chicken. Let stand for 10 minutes.

Place chicken and peppers on greased grill over medium-high heat; close lid and grill, turning chicken once, until no longer pink inside, about 10 minutes. Transfer to cutting board; let cool for 2 minutes. Cut chicken and peppers into ¼-inch (5 mm) thick strips.

Meanwhile, stack tortillas and wrap in double layer of foil. Place on grill over medium heat; close lid and warm through, about 4 minutes. To serve, divide chicken, peppers, lettuce and mozzarella cheese among tortillas; fold up.

Makes 4 servings. PER SERVING: about 398 cal, 39 g pro, 14 g total fat (4 g sat. fat), 36 g carb, 4 g fibre, 82 mg chol, 672 mg sodium. % RDI: 22% calcium, 16% iron, 17% vit A, 62% vit C, 19% folate.

Pico de Gallo

Top your fajitas with this fresh, no-cook traditional Mexican salsa. It's tasty on tacos, salads and nachos, too.

3 cups diced **grape tomatoes,** cherry tomatoes or seeded plum tomatoes

¾ cup finely diced **white onion** or red onion

¼ cup chopped **fresh cilantro**

2 tbsp **lime juice**

1 tbsp minced **jalapeño pepper**

¼ tsp **salt**

In bowl, stir together tomatoes, onion, cilantro, lime juice, jalapeño pepper and salt. Let stand for 30 minutes. *(Make-ahead: Cover and refrigerate for up to 12 hours.)*

Makes 3 cups. PER 1 TBSP: about 3 cal, trace pro, 0 g total fat (0 g sat. fat), 1 g carb, trace fibre, 0 mg chol, 13 mg sodium. % RDI: 1% vit A, 3% vit C, 1% folate.

light &
lively

Chicken Chili Burritos

These burritos are still a bit of an indulgence, but ground chicken lightens up the filling and tastes just as good as ground beef. For a fibre boost, switch to whole wheat or whole grain tortillas.

2 tbsp **vegetable oil**

1 lb (450 g) **ground chicken**

1 **onion,** chopped

2 cloves **garlic,** minced

2 tsp **dried oregano**

½ tsp **salt**

2 tbsp **tomato paste**

1 can (28 oz/796 mL) **diced tomatoes**

3 tbsp **chili powder**

4 **large flour tortillas**

¾ cup shredded **Cheddar cheese**

In large saucepan, heat 1 tbsp of the oil over medium-high heat; cook chicken, breaking up with spoon, until no longer pink, about 8 minutes. Drain fat from pan. Transfer chicken to bowl and set aside.

In same saucepan, heat remaining oil over medium heat; cook onion, garlic, oregano and salt until softened, about 3 minutes. Stir in tomato paste; cook for 1 minute.

Return chicken to pan. Add tomatoes and chili powder; bring to boil. Reduce heat to medium; simmer, stirring occasionally, until thickened, about 15 minutes.

Spoon chili onto centre of each tortilla; sprinkle with Cheddar cheese. Fold in bottom and sides; roll up. Place, seam side down, on greased baking sheet.

Broil burritos, about 6 inches (15 cm) from heat, until crisp and golden, about 10 minutes.

Makes 4 to 6 servings. PER EACH OF 6 SERVINGS: about 427 cal, 24 g pro, 21 g total fat (6 g sat. fat), 38 g carb, 5 g fibre, 64 mg chol, 772 mg sodium. % RDI: 18% calcium, 33% iron, 19% vit A, 37% vit C, 37% folate.

guilt-free fast food

Pork With Spicy-Sweet Pepper Sauce for Two

Pork tenderloin is a lean cut and is the perfect size for an intimate meal for two.
A little crusty bread on the side is great for dipping into the savoury sauce.

1 **pork tenderloin** (14 oz/400 g)

1 clove **garlic,** minced

¼ tsp grated **fresh ginger**

¼ tsp each **salt** and **pepper**

2 tsp **vegetable oil**

SAUCE:

2 tsp **vegetable oil**

Quarter **sweet red pepper,** sliced

1 **red finger hot pepper,** coarsely sliced

1 clove **garlic,** minced

3 tbsp **smooth Thai chili garlic sauce**
   (see Tip, below)

1 tbsp packed **brown sugar**

1 tbsp each **unseasoned rice vinegar** and
   sodium-reduced soy sauce

1 tsp minced **fresh ginger**

1 **green onion,** chopped

Sprinkle pork with garlic, ginger, salt and pepper; let stand for 10 minutes.

In ovenproof skillet, heat oil over medium-high heat; sear pork all over, about 5 minutes.

Transfer to 400°F (200°C) oven; roast until juices run clear when pork is pierced and just a hint of pink remains inside, 15 to 20 minutes. Transfer to cutting board and tent with foil; let stand for 5 minutes before slicing.

SAUCE: Meanwhile, in small saucepan, heat oil over medium heat; cook sweet pepper, hot pepper and garlic until softened, about 3 minutes. Stir in chili sauce, brown sugar, vinegar, soy sauce and ginger; simmer, stirring, until reduced to ½ cup, about 4 minutes. Stir in green onion. Serve over pork slices.

Makes 2 servings. PER SERVING: about 401 cal, 45 g pro, 13 g total fat (2 g sat. fat), 22 g carb, 1 g fibre, 107 mg chol, 863 mg sodium, 803 mg potassium. % RDI: 3% calcium, 21% iron, 9% vit A, 90% vit C, 10% folate.

best
TIPS
ever

There are many different kinds of Thai chili sauce. Some are chunky, with bits of garlic and hot pepper seeds visible in the mix, while others are smoother, blended sauces. Experiment with different brands and types to find the flavour that suits your palate.

Breaded Fish Fingers With Sweet Potato Oven-Fries

This dish is so delicious, you'll never miss the deep-frying. Plus, the sweet potatoes give you a nice vitamin boost.

4 **catfish fillets,** tilapia fillets or
    basa fish fillets (about 6 oz/170 g each)
⅓ cup **light mayonnaise**
¾ cup **dried bread crumbs**
1 tbsp minced **fresh parsley**
1½ tsp **Cajun seasoning**

SWEET POTATO OVEN-FRIES:

2 **sweet potatoes** (about 1½ lb/675 g total)
1 **egg white**
2 tsp **vegetable oil**
¼ tsp each **salt** and **pepper**

SWEET POTATO OVEN-FRIES: Peel sweet potatoes. Cut lengthwise into ½-inch (1 cm) thick slices; cut each slice lengthwise into ½-inch (1 cm) wide strips. Trim to about 3 inches (8 cm) long.

In large bowl, whisk egg white until frothy; whisk in oil, salt and pepper. Add potatoes, tossing to coat. Bake on parchment paper–lined rimmed baking sheet in 450°F (230°C) oven, turning once, until tender and edges are browned and crisp, about 30 minutes.

Meanwhile, cut fish into 3- x 1½-inch (8 x 4 cm) fingers; place in large bowl. Add mayonnaise; toss to coat. In shallow dish, combine bread crumbs, parsley and Cajun seasoning; dip fish into bread crumb mixture, turning to coat.

Bake on greased rimmed baking sheet in 450°F (230°C) oven, turning once, until dark golden and fish flakes easily when tested, about 15 minutes. Serve with fries.

Makes 4 servings. PER SERVING: about 499 cal, 33 g pro, 21 g total fat (4 g sat. fat), 44 g carb, 6 g fibre, 85 mg chol, 542 mg sodium. % RDI: 10% calcium, 21% iron, 293% vit A, 52% vit C, 20% folate.

Spinach Salad With Chicken & Fruit

This dinner salad has it all: veggies, fruit, protein and a savoury homemade dressing. It makes a filling, complete meal for a busy weeknight.

6 cups **fresh baby spinach**

2 cups trimmed **watercress**

1 **boneless skinless chicken breast,** cooked and sliced

½ cup **fresh raspberries**

½ cup **fresh blackberries**

½ cup thinly sliced **red onion**

⅓ cup **slivered almonds**

Half **mango,** peeled and chopped

MINT POPPY SEED DRESSING:

2 tbsp chopped **fresh mint**

2 tbsp **extra-virgin olive oil**

2 tbsp **canola oil**

2 tbsp **red wine vinegar**

1 tbsp minced **shallot**

1 small clove **garlic,** minced

1 tsp **poppy seeds**

Pinch each **salt** and **pepper**

In large bowl, toss together spinach, watercress, chicken, raspberries, blackberries, onion, almonds and mango.

MINT POPPY SEED DRESSING: Whisk together mint, olive oil, canola oil, vinegar, shallot, garlic, poppy seeds, salt and pepper; drizzle over salad and toss to coat.

Makes 4 servings. PER SERVING: about 271 cal, 13 g pro, 19 g total fat (2 g sat. fat), 14 g carb, 5 g fibre, 21 mg chol, 65 mg sodium. % RDI: 11% calcium, 19% iron, 62% vit A, 62% vit C, 51% folate.

quick light mains

Soba Noodles With Pea Shoots & Shiitakes This is a great vegetarian main-course salad or side dish served with grilled meat. Since pea shoots are not as tender as pea tendrils, they need to be cooked before eating.

1 pkg (8 oz/225 g) **soba noodles**
(see Tips, below)

1 tbsp each **sesame oil** and
vegetable oil

2 cloves **garlic,** minced

10 oz (280 g) **shiitake mushrooms,**
stemmed and sliced

12 oz (340 g) **snow pea shoots,**
(about 8 cups), see Tips, below

⅓ cup **light mayonnaise**

¼ cup **sodium-reduced soy sauce**

1 tbsp **unseasoned rice vinegar**

1 tsp **granulated sugar**

1 tsp **sambal oelek** or hot sauce (optional)

In large pot of boiling water, cook soba noodles according to package instructions until tender. Drain and rinse under cold water; drain well and transfer to large bowl.

In wok or large skillet, heat half each of the sesame and vegetable oils over medium-high heat; sauté garlic until fragrant, about 15 seconds. Add mushrooms; sauté until tender, about 4 minutes. Add to noodles.

In wok, heat remaining oils; stir-fry pea shoots until wilted and tender, about 5 minutes. Add to noodle mixture.

Whisk together mayonnaise, soy sauce, vinegar, sugar, and sambal oelek (if using); pour over noodle mixture, tossing to coat. Serve at room temperature or chilled.

Makes 6 servings. PER SERVING: about 247 cal, 10 g pro, 10 g total fat (1 g sat. fat), 34 g carb, 4 g fibre, 5 mg chol, 523 mg sodium, 186 mg potassium. % RDI: 1% calcium, 8% iron, 21% vit A, 47% vit C, 18% folate.

best **TIPS** ever

- Look for soba noodles in the sushi or Asian sections of natural food and grocery stores.

- Snow pea shoots aren't in season for long, so make this dish often when you can find them. They are a beloved springtime treat in Chinese and Japanese cooking; check Asian grocery stores to see if they're in stock.

Broiled Tilapia With Parsley Potatoes & Carrots
This complete supper is ready in about half an hour.

4 **tilapia fillets** or catfish fillets
  (about 6 oz/170 g each)

1 tbsp **extra-virgin olive oil**

½ tsp **salt**

¼ tsp **pepper**

Half **onion,** minced

1 tbsp minced **fresh dill** (or 1 tsp dried dillweed)

Lemon wedges

PARSLEY POTATOES & CARROTS:

8 small **new potatoes** (about 1 lb/450 g total),
  scrubbed

2 **carrots,** thickly sliced

1 tbsp minced **fresh parsley**

1 tbsp **butter**

¼ tsp each **salt** and **pepper**

PARSLEY POTATOES & CARROTS: In saucepan of boiling salted water, cover and cook potatoes for 10 minutes. Add carrots; cook until potatoes are fork-tender, about 10 minutes. Drain and return to pan over low heat, shaking pan until vegetables are dry, about 30 seconds. Add parsley, butter, salt and pepper; toss to coat.

Meanwhile, arrange fish on foil-lined rimmed baking sheet or greased broiler pan; brush with oil. Sprinkle with salt and pepper, then onion and dill. Broil, 6 inches (15 cm) from heat, until fish flakes easily when tested, about 8 minutes. Serve with potatoes and carrots, and squeeze of lemon.

Makes 4 servings. PER SERVING: about 322 cal, 32 g pro, 11 g total fat (3 g sat. fat), 24 g carb, 3 g fibre, 87 mg chol, 942 mg sodium. % RDI: 3% calcium, 10% iron, 112% vit A, 23% vit C, 12% folate.

Orange-Glazed Pork Chops
Tender, juicy pork chops with a sweet orange glaze are on the table in 10 minutes flat. Serve with brown rice and a green vegetable.

4 **bone-in pork loin centre chops**
  (1½ lb/675 g total)

¼ tsp each **salt** and **pepper**

1 tsp **vegetable oil**

3 cloves **garlic,** minced

½ tsp crumbled **dried sage**

¾ cup **chicken broth**

½ cup **orange juice**

1 tbsp **cornstarch**

1 **green onion,** chopped

1 **orange,** cut in wedges

Trim fat from chops; sprinkle with salt and pepper. In large nonstick skillet, heat oil over medium-high heat; brown chops. Transfer to plate.

Drain fat from pan; cook garlic and sage over medium heat, stirring, until fragrant, 30 seconds. Add broth and orange juice, stirring and scraping up browned bits from bottom of pan. Return chops and any accumulated juices to pan.

Stir cornstarch with 1 tbsp cold water; stir into pan. Cook until thickened and just a hint of pink remains inside pork, about 2 minutes. Sprinkle with green onion; garnish with orange wedges.

Makes 4 servings. PER SERVING: about 245 cal, 25 g pro, 11 g total fat (4 g sat. fat), 10 g carb, 1 g fibre, 69 mg chol, 347 mg sodium. % RDI: 4% calcium, 9% iron, 1% vit A, 47% vit C, 11% folate.

Curried Lentil, Wild Rice & Orzo Salad A wonderful

mix of textures, this gently spiced salad goes with all sorts of mains. It holds up well in the fridge, so you can make it up to a day ahead of serving.

½ cup **wild rice**

⅔ cup **dried green lentils** or
   dried brown lentils

½ cup **orzo pasta**

½ cup **dried currants**

¼ cup finely chopped **red onion**

⅓ cup **slivered almonds,** toasted

DRESSING:

¼ cup **white wine vinegar**

1 tsp **ground cumin**

1 tsp **Dijon mustard**

½ tsp each **granulated sugar, salt**
   and **ground coriander**

¼ tsp each **turmeric, sweet paprika** and
   nutmeg

Pinch each **cinnamon, ground cloves** and
   cayenne pepper

⅓ cup **canola oil** or vegetable oil

In large pot of boiling salted water, cover and cook wild rice for 10 minutes. Add lentils; cook for 20 minutes.

Add orzo; cook just until tender, about 5 minutes. Drain well and transfer to large bowl. Add currants and onion.

DRESSING: In small bowl, whisk together vinegar, cumin, mustard, sugar, salt, coriander, turmeric, paprika, nutmeg, cinnamon, cloves and cayenne pepper; whisk in oil. Pour over rice mixture and gently toss to coat.

Let cool. Cover and refrigerate until chilled, about 4 hours. *(Make-ahead: Refrigerate for up to 24 hours.)*

To serve, sprinkle salad with almonds.

Makes 12 servings. PER SERVING: about 178 cal, 6 g pro, 8 g total fat (1 g sat. fat), 22 g carb, 3 g fibre, 0 mg chol, 178 mg sodium, 231 mg potassium. % RDI: 2% calcium, 13% iron, 2% vit C, 30% folate.

superfood
salads

Broccoli Salad

Vitamin-rich broccoli gets all dressed up for a party in this vibrant salad. None of the ingredients will wilt, so this make-and-take dish is also a tasty option for potlucks, picnics and lunches.

4 cups sliced **broccoli stems and florets**

Half **sweet red pepper,** chopped

½ cup chopped **red onion** or sweet onion

¼ cup cubed **feta cheese**

2 tbsp **unsalted hulled sunflower seeds**

2 tbsp **extra-virgin olive oil**

1 tbsp **red wine vinegar**

¼ tsp each **salt** and **pepper**

In saucepan of boiling salted water, cover and cook broccoli until tender-crisp, about 2 minutes. Drain and chill in cold water; drain well.

In bowl, combine broccoli, red pepper, red onion, feta cheese and sunflower seeds. Stir together oil, vinegar, salt and pepper; pour over salad. Toss to coat. *(Make-ahead: Cover and refrigerate for up to 24 hours.)*

Makes 4 servings. PER SERVING: about 153 cal, 5 g pro, 12 g total fat (3 g sat. fat), 10 g carb, 3 g fibre, 9 mg chol, 493 mg sodium, 353 mg potassium. % RDI: 8% calcium, 9% iron, 20% vit A, 128% vit C, 55% folate.

Mixed Greens With Tuna & Pumpkin Seeds

This pretty supper salad works for a family dinner or for entertaining. Pepitas, or hulled raw pumpkin seeds, are full of minerals and add a nice crunch to recipes.

4 **pitas**

6 cups torn **mixed greens**

1 large **tomato,** sliced

2 cans **solid white tuna** or chunk light tuna, drained (see Tips, below)

¼ cup **unsalted pepitas**

DRESSING:

½ cup **extra-virgin olive oil**

¼ cup **balsamic vinegar**

2 small cloves **garlic,** minced

1½ tsp chopped **fresh rosemary** (see Tips, below)

¼ tsp each **salt** and **pepper**

DRESSING: Whisk together oil, vinegar, garlic, rosemary, salt and pepper.

Brush pitas with 1 tbsp of the dressing. Place on greased grill or grill pan over medium-high heat; close lid and grill, turning once, until crisp, about 4 minutes. Cut into quarters.

In large bowl, toss greens with ¼ cup of the remaining dressing. Divide among plates; place tomato slices around edges. Break tuna into chunks; sprinkle over greens. Sprinkle with pumpkin seeds and drizzle with remaining dressing. Serve with pitas.

Makes 4 servings. PER SERVING: about 575 cal, 25 g pro, 34 g total fat (5 g sat. fat), 42 g carb, 4 g fibre, 28 mg chol, 747 mg sodium, 677 mg potassium. % RDI: 12% calcium, 33% iron, 22% vit A, 30% vit C, 56% folate.

best
TIPS
ever

- To boost your intake of omega-3 fatty acids, you can substitute canned sardines or salmon for the tuna.

- If you don't have any rosemary on hand to make the dressing, basil, thyme or chervil are nice substitutes.

Chicken With 40 Cloves of Garlic

Garlic is great for your heart, and this skillet version of a classic French oven-braised chicken offers plenty of it. To make peeling easier, lay garlic cloves in groups of four on a cutting board and press down with the side of a chef's knife to loosen the skins.

1 tbsp **vegetable oil**

8 **chicken thighs** (2 lb/900 g total), skinned

40 cloves **garlic** (about 4 heads)

½ tsp crumbled **dried thyme**

½ tsp crumbled **dried rosemary**

¼ tsp crumbled **dried sage**

¼ tsp **pepper**

Pinch **salt**

1 tbsp **all-purpose flour**

1 cup **chicken broth**

2 tbsp minced **fresh parsley**

In large skillet, heat oil over medium-high heat; brown chicken all over. Transfer to plate.

Drain fat from pan; fry garlic, thyme, rosemary, sage, pepper and salt over medium heat until garlic is golden, about 5 minutes. Sprinkle with flour; cook, stirring, for 1 minute. Add broth and bring to boil, scraping up browned bits from bottom of pan; reduce heat and simmer for 5 minutes.

Return chicken and any accumulated juices to pan; cover and simmer, turning once, until juices run clear when chicken is pierced and garlic is softened, about 25 minutes. *(Make-ahead: Refrigerate in airtight container for up to 24 hours or freeze for up to 1 month. Reheat before continuing.)* Sprinkle with parsley.

Makes 4 servings. PER SERVING: about 298 cal, 33 g pro, 12 g total fat (3 g sat. fat), 12 g carb, 1 g fibre, 116 mg chol, 297 mg sodium. % RDI: 7% calcium, 21% iron, 4% vit A, 17% vit C, 8% folate.

change it up

Slow Cooker Chicken With 40 Cloves of Garlic: Do not remove chicken skin. After browning chicken, transfer to slow cooker. Continue with recipe but omit flour, scraping broth mixture into slow cooker. Cover and cook on low for 4 hours. Skim off any fat. Whisk ¼ cup water with 3 tbsp all-purpose flour and stir into slow cooker; cover and cook on high until thickened, about 15 minutes. Remove chicken skin if desired. Sprinkle with parsley.

heart-healthy mains

Chickpea Patties in Pitas With Cilantro Yogurt

Legumes such as chickpeas are high in fibre and protein, are low in fat and contain no cholesterol. They're an essential part of vegetarian diets, but they're so yummy – especially in these seasoned patties – that even meat eaters love them.

2 cans (19 oz/540 mL each) **chickpeas,**
  drained and rinsed

2 **eggs**

2 tbsp **Cajun seasoning**

½ tsp each **salt** and **pepper**

¼ cup **fresh bread crumbs**
  (see Tip, below)

3 **green onions,** thinly sliced

2 cloves **garlic,** minced

3 tbsp **vegetable oil**

3 **large whole wheat pitas**

1½ cups shredded **carrots**

1½ cups thinly sliced **English cucumber**

CILANTRO YOGURT:

½ cup **plain yogurt**

2 tbsp chopped **fresh cilantro** or
  fresh mint

CILANTRO YOGURT: Mix yogurt with cilantro; set aside.

In food processor, pulse together chickpeas, eggs, Cajun seasoning, salt and pepper until smooth; transfer to bowl. Add bread crumbs, green onions, garlic and 2 tbsp of the cilantro yogurt; stir to combine. With wet hands, shape into six ½-inch (1 cm) thick patties. *(Make-ahead: Cover and refrigerate patties and yogurt separately for up to 24 hours.)*

In large nonstick skillet, heat oil over medium heat; fry patties, turning once, until golden and crisp, 10 minutes.

Cut each pita in half; stuff each pocket with 1 of the patties. Spread remaining cilantro yogurt over patties; top with carrots and cucumber.

Makes 6 servings. PER SERVING: about 391 cal, 15 g pro, 12 g total fat (2 g sat. fat), 59 g carb, 10 g fibre, 64 mg chol, 904 mg sodium. % RDI: 11% calcium, 27% iron, 89% vit A, 17% vit C, 57% folate.

best
TIPS ever

Fresh bread crumbs are so easy to make in a food processor. Cut bread into chunks, then pulse until fine and crumbly. They freeze well too, so make them whenever you have a leftover piece of baguette or other crusty bread.

Chili-Roasted Salmon

Here's a scrumptious way to get hearty-healthy omega-3 fats. This salmon is stylish and ready in just 15 minutes.

4 **skin-on centre-cut salmon fillets**
   (1½ lb/675 g total)

1 tbsp **vegetable oil**

1½ tsp **chili powder**

½ tsp **salt**

2 tbsp chopped **fresh cilantro** or
   fresh parsley

1 **lime,** cut in wedges

Place fish, skin side down, on foil-lined rimmed baking sheet. Whisk together oil, chili powder and salt: spread over fish. Roast in 450°F (230°C) oven until fish flakes easily when tested, about 10 minutes per inch (2.5 cm) of thickness.

Slide metal spatula between flesh and skin to transfer to plates. Sprinkle with cilantro; serve with lime wedges to squeeze over top

Makes 4 servings. PER SERVING: about 255 cal, 31 g pro, 13 g total fat (2 g sat. fat), 1 g carb, trace fibre, 85 mg chol, 364 mg sodium. % RDI: 2% calcium, 10% iron, 5% vit A, 5% vit C, 16% folate.

Green Bean & Barley Salad

Fibre-rich pot barley is a totally tasty partner with crunchy fresh green beans in this side.

1 lb (450 g) **green beans**

1 cup **pot barley** or pearl barley

¼ cup **extra-virgin olive oil**

3 tbsp **white wine vinegar**

1 clove **garlic,** minced

1½ tsp minced **fresh thyme**

1½ tsp **Dijon mustard**

½ tsp **salt**

¼ tsp **pepper**

4 cups **baby arugula**

2 cups **grape tomatoes** or
   cherry tomatoes, halved

2 **green onions,** thinly sliced

⅔ cup crumbled **feta cheese**

Trim beans; halve diagonally. In saucepan of boiling water, blanch beans until tender-crisp, about 3 minutes. Chill in ice water; drain and pat dry.

Meanwhile, in pot of boiling salted water, cook barley until tender, 20 to 25 minutes. Drain; let cool for 5 minutes.

In large bowl, whisk together oil, vinegar, garlic, thyme, mustard, salt and pepper; add beans and barley, tossing to coat well.

Add arugula, tomatoes and green onions, tossing well. *(Make-ahead: Cover and let stand for up to 1 hour or refrigerate for up to 4 hours.)* Stir in feta cheese.

Makes 12 servings. PER SERVING: about 142 cal, 4 g pro, 7 g total fat (2 g sat. fat), 18 g carb, 3 g fibre, 8 mg chol, 254 mg sodium, 231 mg potassium. % RDI: 9% calcium, 9% iron, 10% vit A, 17% vit C, 20% folate.

Turkey & Rapini Fusilli

Lean turkey adds healthy protein to this vegetable-packed, gluten-free pasta. Blanching the rapini gets rid of some of its characteristic bitterness. You may be tempted to blanch it in the same pot as the pasta, but don't: The bitter taste will transfer.

1 tbsp **olive oil**

8 oz (225 g) **extra-lean ground turkey**

½ tsp **poultry seasoning**

1½ cups diced **fennel bulb** (about half bulb)

3 cloves **garlic,** thinly sliced

Pinch **hot pepper flakes** (optional)

8 oz (225 g) **brown rice fusilli**

12 oz (340 g) **rapini,** cut in 1-inch (2.5 cm) pieces

1 tbsp **lemon juice**

¼ tsp **salt**

Pinch **pepper**

¼ cup grated **Parmesan cheese**

In large nonstick skillet, heat 1 tsp of the oil over medium-high heat; cook turkey and poultry seasoning, breaking up with spoon, until no longer pink, about 3 minutes. Transfer to plate; set aside.

Drain fat from pan; wipe clean. Heat remaining oil over medium heat; cook fennel, garlic, and hot pepper flakes (if using) until fennel is softened, about 5 minutes. Return turkey and any accumulated juices to pan.

Meanwhile, in pot of boiling lightly salted water, cook pasta according to package directions until al dente. Reserving ⅓ cup of the cooking liquid, drain pasta.

In separate pot of boiling lightly salted water, blanch rapini until tender, about 2 minutes.

Add pasta, rapini, reserved cooking liquid, lemon juice, salt and pepper to turkey mixture; cook, stirring, until coated, about 1 minute.

Remove from heat; sprinkle with Parmesan cheese.

Makes 4 servings. PER SERVING: about 347 cal, 20 g pro, 9 g total fat (3 g sat. fat), 51 g carb, 4 g fibre, 50 mg chol, 755 mg sodium, 548 mg potassium. % RDI: 17% calcium, 27% iron, 21% vit A, 30% vit C, 30% folate.

lower-calorie mains

Pan-Fried Steak With Horseradish Rutabaga Mash

Rutabaga, also (mistakenly) called turnip, is often overlooked. This root vegetable is similar in texture to potatoes and is delicious mashed or roasted. It is available year-round and stays fresh thanks to its waxy skin.

1 lb (450 g) **beef top sirloin grilling steak**

½ tsp **smoked paprika**

¼ tsp each **salt** and **pepper**

1 tsp **vegetable oil**

HORSERADISH RUTABAGA MASH:

1 **rutabaga** (about 1¾ lb/790 g), peeled and cubed

2 cloves **garlic**

1 lb (450 g) **russet potatoes,** peeled and cubed

¼ cup **light sour cream**

2 tbsp **prepared horseradish**

½ tsp **salt**

¼ tsp **pepper**

¼ cup chopped **fresh chives**

HORSERADISH RUTABAGA MASH: In pot of boiling salted water, cook rutabaga and garlic for 15 minutes; add potatoes. Cook until rutabaga is fork-tender, about 10 minutes; drain. In food processor, pulse together rutabaga, garlic, potatoes, sour cream, horseradish, salt and pepper until smooth. Stir in chives.

Meanwhile, rub steak all over with paprika, salt and pepper. In cast-iron or nonstick skillet, heat oil over medium-high heat; fry steak, turning once, until medium-rare, 4 to 8 minutes. Transfer to cutting board; let stand, uncovered, for 5 minutes. Slice across the grain. Serve with mash.

Makes 4 servings. PER SERVING: about 307 cal, 28 g pro, 7 g total fat (3 g sat. fat), 34 g carb, 5 g fibre, 55 mg chol, 923 mg sodium, 1,371 mg potassium. % RDI: 12% calcium, 29% iron, 12% vit A, 78% vit C, 20% folate.

Lemongrass Pork Tenderloin With Stir-Fried Quinoa

White rice and fatty pork chops are replaced with protein-packed quinoa and lean pork tenderloin in this twist on a Vietnamese favourite. Serve it with cooked greens, such as spinach or bok choy.

1 stalk **lemongrass**

2 **green onions,** sliced

2 cloves **garlic**

1 tbsp packed **brown sugar**

1 tbsp **fish sauce**

1 tbsp **unseasoned rice vinegar**

1 lb (450 g) **pork tenderloin**

1 tsp **vegetable oil**

STIR-FRIED QUINOA:

1 tbsp **vegetable oil**

3 cloves **garlic,** minced

1 tsp minced **fresh ginger**

1 tsp **ground coriander**

8 cups sliced **Swiss chard leaves**
    and **stems** (about 1 bunch)

3 cups cold **cooked quinoa** (about
    1 cup uncooked), see Tips, below

½ tsp each **salt** and **pepper**

PICKLED RADISH SALAD:

2 tbsp **unseasoned rice vinegar**

1 tsp **granulated sugar**

Pinch **salt**

1 cup julienned **carrot**

1 cup julienned **daikon radish**
    (see Tips, below)

Trim dry ends off lemongrass and discard tough outer leaves; slice lemongrass. In blender, purée together lemongrass, green onions, garlic, ¼ cup water, brown sugar, fish sauce and vinegar to form thin paste.

Trim any fat or silverskin off pork; place pork in shallow dish. Pour lemongrass mixture over top, turning to coat; cover and refrigerate for 2 hours. (*Make-ahead: Refrigerate for up to 24 hours.*)

PICKLED RADISH SALAD: Meanwhile, in bowl, whisk together vinegar, sugar and salt; stir in carrot and daikon radish. Cover and refrigerate for 2 hours. (*Make-ahead: Refrigerate for up to 24 hours.*)

In large nonstick skillet, heat oil over medium-high heat; brown pork all over, about 8 minutes. Transfer to foil-lined baking sheet; bake in 375°F (190°C) oven until juices run clear when pork is pierced and just a hint of pink remains inside, or instant-read thermometer inserted into thickest part reads 160°F (71°C), about 35 minutes.

Transfer pork to cutting board; tent with foil and let stand for 5 minutes before slicing.

STIR-FRIED QUINOA: Meanwhile, in large nonstick skillet or wok, heat oil over medium-high heat; cook garlic, ginger and coriander until fragrant, about 1 minute. Add Swiss chard; cook until wilted, about 2 minutes. Add quinoa, salt and pepper; cook, stirring occasionally, until heated through, about 5 minutes.

Serve quinoa topped with pork and radish salad.

Makes 6 servings. PER SERVING: about 222 cal, 21 g pro, 6 g total fat (1 g sat. fat), 23 g carb, 3 g fibre, 41 mg chol, 560 mg sodium, 791 mg potassium. % RDI: 6% calcium, 29% iron, 52% vit A, 25% vit C, 14% folate.

best
TIPS
ever

• Daikon radish has a very pungent aroma, but it's crunchy and sweet, and lends itself well to pickling. If it's not your thing, you can substitute the same amount of carrot.

• This recipe is a great way to use up leftover quinoa; if you don't have any on hand, make it ahead and spread it out on a large rimmed baking sheet to cool quickly.

Grilled Chicken Barley Salad

Barley has a pleasantly chewy texture, which livens up this all-in-one dinner salad. Try the easy vinaigrette on green salads and steamed vegetables too.

2 **boneless skinless chicken breasts**

⅔ cup **pearl barley**

1½ cups chopped trimmed **green beans**

1 cup **grape tomatoes,** halved

¼ cup finely minced **red onion**

2 tbsp chopped **fresh basil**

VINAIGRETTE:

¼ cup **extra-virgin olive oil**

2 tbsp **wine vinegar**

1 tbsp **Dijon mustard**

½ tsp **dried Italian herb seasoning**

¼ tsp each **salt** and **pepper**

VINAIGRETTE: In large bowl, whisk together oil, vinegar, mustard, Italian herb seasoning, salt and pepper. Transfer 2 tbsp to large shallow dish; add chicken, turning to coat. Cover and refrigerate for 10 minutes. *(Make-ahead: Refrigerate for up to 8 hours.)*

Meanwhile, in saucepan of boiling water, cover and cook barley for 10 minutes. Add green beans; cook until beans are tender-crisp and barley is tender, about 10 minutes. Drain and toss with remaining vinaigrette.

Place chicken on greased grill over medium-high heat; close lid and grill, turning once, until no longer pink inside, about 10 minutes. Cut into cubes.

Add chicken to barley mixture. Add tomatoes, onion and basil; toss to combine.

Makes 4 servings. PER SERVING: about 340 cal, 19 g pro, 15 g total fat (2 g sat. fat), 33 g carb, 4 g fibre, 39 mg chol, 236 mg sodium. % RDI: 4% calcium, 16% iron, 7% vit A, 13% vit C, 16% folate.

more healthy chicken mains

Tandoori Chicken With a jar

of fragrant Tandoori Spice Blend (right) on hand, an exotic dinner is only an hour away. Serve with naan or rice.

½ cup **plain yogurt**

1 tbsp **Tandoori Spice Blend** (right)

1 tbsp minced **fresh ginger**

2 cloves **garlic,** minced

8 **chicken drumsticks,** skinned

1 tbsp **vegetable oil**

In large glass bowl, stir together yogurt, Tandoori Spice Blend, ginger and garlic; add chicken, turning to coat. Cover and refrigerate for 30 minutes. *(Make-ahead: Refrigerate for up to 24 hours.)*

Arrange chicken on foil-lined rimmed baking sheet; drizzle oil over top. Bake in 400°F (200°C) oven until juices run clear when chicken is pierced, about 30 minutes. Broil until browned and crisp, about 3 minutes.

Makes 4 servings. PER SERVING: about 200 cal, 25 g pro, 9 g total fat (2 g sat. fat), 4 g carb, 1 g fibre, 97 mg chol, 290 mg sodium, 398 mg potassium. % RDI: 7% calcium, 15% iron, 3% vit A, 7% vit C, 5% folate.

Tandoori Spice Blend

Toasting the seeds, cinnamon and cloves before blending them with other spices awakens their flavours and aromas.

⅓ cup **cumin seeds**

⅓ cup **coriander seeds**

1 stick **cinnamon,** broken in chunks

1 tbsp **whole cloves**

1 tbsp each **ground ginger, turmeric** and
   mace

1 tbsp **salt**

1 tbsp **garlic powder**

1 tsp **cayenne pepper**

In dry small heavy skillet, toast cumin, coriander, cinnamon and cloves over medium heat, stirring, until fragrant and slightly darkened, 2 to 3 minutes. Let cool.

Transfer to spice grinder or clean coffee grinder (wipe coffee grinder with paper towel before and after use); add ginger, turmeric, mace, salt, garlic powder and cayenne pepper. Grind together. *(Make-ahead: Store in airtight container for up to 1 month.)*

Makes about ¾ cup.

Chicken Braised With Lemon, Fennel & Garlic

Garlic becomes sweet as it cooks gently in this fennel-scented broth. The fennel fronds have a delicate flavour similar to dill, which adds even more depth to the dish. Serve with creamy mashed potatoes and steamed asparagus.

1 bulb **fennel** (about 1 lb/450 g)

⅓ cup **all-purpose flour**

¼ tsp each **salt** and **pepper**

12 **boneless skinless chicken thighs**
(about 2 lb/900 g total),
see Tip, below

2 tbsp **vegetable oil**

20 large cloves **garlic** (about 2 heads),
peeled

2 cups **chicken broth**

1 cup **white wine**

Half **lemon,** thinly sliced

2 tbsp chopped **fresh dill**

Cut fennel in half lengthwise and core; cut lengthwise into ¼-inch (5 mm) thick slices. Chop fennel fronds. Set aside.

In shallow dish, combine flour, salt and pepper; dredge chicken in flour mixture to coat all over. Reserve remaining flour mixture.

In large shallow Dutch oven, heat oil over medium-high heat; brown chicken, in batches. Transfer to plate. Drain fat from pan; cook garlic over medium heat, stirring, until golden, about 1 minute.

Add broth and wine; bring to boil, stirring and scraping up browned bits. Add lemon and sliced fennel; return chicken and any accumulated juices to pan. Reduce heat, cover and simmer until juices run clear when chicken is pierced, about 30 minutes. Transfer chicken, lemon and fennel to platter; cover and keep warm.

In bowl, whisk reserved flour mixture with ¼ cup cold water; whisk into pan and boil over medium-high heat, whisking, until thickened, about 5 minutes. Stir in chopped fennel fronds and dill; pour over chicken.

Makes 6 servings. PER SERVING: about 315 cal, 33 g pro, 13 g total fat (2 g sat. fat), 14 g carb, 3 g fibre, 125 mg chol, 518 mg sodium. % RDI: 7% calcium, 21% iron, 3% vit A, 30% vit C, 14% folate.

best
TIPS
ever

It's tempting to swap in leaner chicken breasts for the thighs, but braising can give chicken breasts an unpleasant, stringy texture. This dish still falls well within the normal daily allotment of calories and fat, so enjoy its rich flavours.

Cioppino

For the best flavour in this West Coast classic, use the freshest seafood you can find. Cut scallops in half if they are more than 1 inch (2.5 cm) thick. Serve with toasted baguette slices to soak up the mouthwatering broth.

1 tbsp **olive oil**

1 small **sweet onion,** diced

4 cloves **garlic,** minced

¼ cup **dry white wine**

1 cup **bottled strained tomatoes** (passata)

1 tsp **dried oregano**

¼ tsp **pepper**

1 bottle (236 mL) **clam juice**

8 oz (225 g) **raw large shrimp,** peeled and deveined

8 oz (225 g) **sea scallops**

8 oz (225 g) **firm white fish fillet** (such as cod or halibut), cut crosswise in strips

In large saucepan, heat oil over medium-high heat; cook onion, stirring occasionally, until softened, about 4 minutes. Add garlic; cook for 1 minute.

Pour in wine; cook, scraping up browned bits, until slightly reduced, about 1 minute. Add tomatoes, oregano, pepper and clam juice; bring to boil. Reduce heat and simmer for 5 minutes.

Stir in shrimp, scallops and fish; cover and cook over medium heat until shrimp are pink, and scallops and fish are opaque, about 5 minutes.

Makes 4 servings. PER SERVING: about 219 cal, 29 g pro, 5 g total fat (1 g sat. fat), 11 g carb, 1 g fibre, 109 mg chol, 438 mg sodium, 801 mg potassium. % RDI: 7% calcium, 22% iron, 4% vit A, 13% vit C, 13% folate.

cut-the-fat mains

Pork Tenderloin With Grilled Cantaloupe

Sure, raw melon is great. But have you ever tried it grilled? The barbecue adds a hint of luscious smoky caramel.

1 **pork tenderloin** (about 1 lb/450 g)

¼ tsp each **salt** and **pepper**

2 tbsp **hot pepper jelly**

2 tsp **orange juice**

½ tsp **Dijon mustard**

Half **cantaloupe**

Trim any fat or silverskin off pork; tuck thin end under and secure with wooden skewer. Sprinkle with salt and pepper.

Place pork on greased grill over medium heat; close lid and grill for 15 minutes, turning to brown all over.

Meanwhile, in small bowl, stir together hot pepper jelly, orange juice and mustard; brush over pork. Grill, covered, until glazed and just a hint of pink remains inside, or instant-read thermometer inserted into thickest part reads 160°F (71°C), about 5 minutes.

Meanwhile, peel and seed cantaloupe; cut into ½-inch (1 cm) thick half-moons. Grill, turning once, until grill-marked, about 5 minutes.

Makes 4 servings. PER SERVING: about 161 cal, 21 g pro, 3 g total fat (1 g sat. fat), 13 g carb, 1 g fibre, 46 mg chol, 198 mg sodium. % RDI: 1% calcium, 9% iron, 16% vit A, 35% vit C, 5% folate.

Mushroom "Steaks"

Portobellos, the "steaks" of mushrooms, are meaty enough to satisfy vegetarians and nonvegetarians alike. They also make a sumptuous side dish.

4 large **portobello mushrooms**
   (2 lb/900 g total)

BARBECUE SAUCE:

⅓ cup **ketchup**

¼ cup minced **red onion**

¼ cup **Dijon mustard**

1 tbsp packed **brown sugar**

1 tbsp **cider vinegar**

1 clove **garlic,** minced

¼ tsp **pepper**

Remove stems from mushrooms and save for another use.

BARBECUE SAUCE: In large bowl, whisk together ketchup, onion, mustard, brown sugar, vinegar, garlic and pepper. Add mushrooms; toss to coat. *(Make-ahead: Cover and refrigerate for up to 24 hours.)*

Place mushrooms on greased grill over medium-high heat; close lid and grill, brushing with remaining sauce and turning once, until browned and tender, about 10 minutes.

Makes 4 servings. PER SERVING: about 97 cal, 5 g pro, 1 g total fat (trace sat. fat), 20 g carb, 3 g fibre, 0 mg chol, 481 mg sodium. % RDI: 4% calcium, 11% iron, 2% vit A, 7% vit C, 13% folate.

Beef & Bulgur Pitas

It's easy to increase the amount of whole grains in your diet by adding them to the stuffing of a savoury pita sandwich. Not only does the bulgur offer valuable nutrients but it means you don't need as much meat to fill up your pita.

½ cup medium or coarse **bulgur** (see Tip, below)

8 oz (225 g) **extra-lean ground beef**

1 each **carrot** and **zucchini,** shredded

1 **onion,** chopped

2 cloves **garlic,** minced

1 tbsp **chili powder**

1 tsp **ground cumin**

¼ tsp **pepper**

1 cup **no-salt-added tomato juice**

½ cup chopped **fresh cilantro** or fresh parsley

2 tsp **lime juice**

4 **whole wheat pitas**

4 leaves **leaf lettuce**

16 slices **English cucumber**

16 **cherry tomatoes,** halved

¼ cup **low-fat plain yogurt**

In saucepan, bring ¾ cup water to boil; stir in bulgur. Reduce heat to low; cover and simmer until no liquid remains, about 10 minutes.

Meanwhile, in nonstick skillet, cook beef over medium-high heat, breaking up with spoon, until no longer pink, about 5 minutes.

Drain any fat from pan. Cook carrot, zucchini, onion, garlic, chili powder, cumin and pepper over medium heat, stirring occasionally, until onion is tender, about 5 minutes. Add tomato juice and bring to boil; reduce heat and simmer until liquid is almost evaporated, about 5 minutes. Stir in bulgur, ¼ cup of the cilantro and lime juice.

Cut top third off each pita; place inside each bottom. Line each with lettuce leaf and some of the cucumber. Spoon in beef mixture; top with tomatoes, remaining cucumber, yogurt and remaining cilantro.

Makes 4 servings. PER SERVING: about 372 cal, 23 g pro, 7 g total fat (2 g sat. fat), 59 g carb, 9 g fibre, 32 mg chol, 413 mg sodium, 818 mg potassium. % RDI: 8% calcium, 35% iron, 60% vit A, 35% vit C, 36% folate.

best
TIPS
ever

Bulgur is made by removing just a small portion of the bran that coats a wheat kernel. Even though it's missing some of that bran, bulgur is still considered a whole grain. Choose from coarse, medium or fine grind, depending on the texture you prefer. Look for it in the health food aisle in supermarkets, bulk stores and Middle Eastern grocery stores.

Brown Butter Trout & Broccoli en Papillote

This fun yet sophisticated French method of baking fish in sealed parchment paper is elegant and makes cleanup easy. If you don't have parchment paper, just use foil instead. Serve with steamed brown rice.

¼ cup **butter**

2 **trout fillets** (about 8 oz/225 g each)

¼ tsp each **salt** and **pepper**

4 slices **lemon**

3 cups bite-size **broccoli florets**

1 **shallot,** thinly sliced

⅓ cup **sliced almonds**

In small skillet, cook butter over medium heat until light brown and fragrant, about 5 minutes. Set aside.

Cut four 14- x 10-inch (35 x 25 cm) pieces of parchment paper. Fold each in half crosswise. Trim corners to make half-heart shape. Unfold to make 4 large hearts.

Cut trout fillets in half crosswise. Place each half on centre of 1 half of each paper heart. Sprinkle each with pinch each salt and pepper; top each with lemon slice. Top with broccoli and shallot; drizzle each with 1 tbsp browned butter. Fold paper over. Starting at rounded end, fold over edge, overlapping and pleating to enclose. Twist pointed end to secure.

Bake packets on large rimmed baking sheet in 400°F (200°C) oven for 11 minutes. Remove from oven; let stand until fish flakes easily when tested, about 5 minutes.

Meanwhile, toast almonds on baking sheet until golden, about 5 minutes.

To serve, cut or tear open packets, being careful to avoid steam. Sprinkle with toasted almonds.

Makes 4 servings. PER SERVING: about 322 cal, 27 g pro, 22 g total fat (9 g sat. fat), 5 g carb, 2 g fibre, 97 mg chol, 282 mg sodium, 759 mg potassium. % RDI: 11% calcium, 8% iron, 34% vit A, 58% vit C, 19% folate.

change it up
Brown Butter Halibut & Zucchini en Papillote: Substitute halibut fillets for the trout and 1 large zucchini, thinly sliced, for the broccoli.

light dinner ideas

Grilled Chicken Niçoise Salad

The quintessential bistro salade Niçoise features tuna. This version has been updated with lean chicken, but it has all the other wonderful flavours of the original.

4 **boneless skinless chicken breasts**
  (1 lb/450 g total)

8 oz (225 g) **green beans,** trimmed

2 **tomatoes,** cut in 8 wedges each

4 cups torn **Boston lettuce** or
  Bibb lettuce

⅓ cup pitted **black olives**

FRENCH DRESSING:

¼ cup **extra-virgin olive oil**

2 tbsp **white wine vinegar**

2 tsp **lemon juice**

1 tsp **granulated sugar**

½ tsp **herbes de Provence** (see Tip, below)
  or dried thyme

½ tsp **sweet paprika**

¼ tsp each **salt** and **pepper**

FRENCH DRESSING: In jar with lid, shake together oil, vinegar, lemon juice, sugar, herbes de Provence, paprika, salt and pepper. Pour 3 tbsp of the dressing into bowl; add chicken and turn to coat. Let stand for 10 minutes.

Place chicken on greased grill over medium-high heat; close lid and grill, turning once, until no longer pink inside, about 12 minutes. Thinly slice.

Meanwhile, in saucepan of boiling salted water, cover and blanch green beans until tender-crisp, about 2 minutes. Drain and chill under cold water; drain well.

In large bowl, toss together green beans, tomatoes, lettuce, olives and remaining dressing; divide salad among plates. Arrange chicken on top.

Makes 4 servings. PER SERVING: about 301 cal, 28 g pro, 17 g total fat (3 g sat. fat), 11 g carb, 3 g fibre, 67 mg chol, 425 mg sodium. % RDI: 6% calcium, 16% iron, 15% vit A, 37% vit C, 32% folate.

best
TIPS
ever

Herbes de Provence is a blend of dried herbs typically used in southern French cuisine. It usually contains savory, fennel seeds, basil and thyme, but some blends include a whole host of other herbs. Many also contain dried lavender, so check the label if that's not your favourite seasoning.

Japanese Cold Noodle "Chef Salad"

You can dress up this perfect summer supper even more with sliced mushrooms or tofu and finely shredded cabbage or carrots. Toast the sesame seeds briefly in a dry skillet.

2 **eggs**

1 tbsp **vegetable oil**

Pinch **salt**

12 oz (340 g) **Chinese wheat noodles** or ramen noodles

2 tsp **sesame oil**

8 oz (225 g) **ham,** julienned

1 **sweet red pepper,** very thinly sliced

1 cup shredded **cucumber**

4 cups shredded **iceberg lettuce**

2 **green onions,** thinly sliced

4 tsp **sesame seeds,** toasted

SAUCE:

⅔ cup **chicken broth**

⅓ cup **granulated sugar**

⅓ cup **unseasoned rice vinegar** or cider vinegar

3 tbsp **soy sauce**

1 tbsp grated **fresh ginger**

SAUCE: In saucepan, bring broth, sugar, vinegar, soy sauce and ginger to boil; reduce heat and simmer for 5 minutes. Strain and refrigerate until cool. *(Make-ahead: Refrigerate in airtight container for up to 3 days.)*

Beat together eggs, 1 tsp of the oil and salt. Heat 6-inch (15 cm) nonstick skillet over medium-high heat; brush lightly with some of the remaining oil. Pour in about one-quarter of the egg mixture, tilting pan to spread evenly; cook until top is set, about 30 seconds. Slide out onto cutting board. Repeat with remaining oil and egg mixture to make 4 thin omelettes; stack and cut into fine shreds.

In large pot of boiling salted water, cook noodles until tender but firm, about 5 minutes. Drain and chill under cold water; drain well. In bowl, toss noodles with sesame oil.

Arrange noodles on 4 dinner plates. Attractively top with eggs, ham, red pepper, cucumber and lettuce. Sprinkle with green onions. *(Make-ahead: Cover and refrigerate up to 4 hours.)*

Sprinkle with sauce and sesame seeds.

Makes 4 servings. PER SERVING: about 696 cal, 27 g pro, 30 g total fat (10 g sat. fat), 81 g carb, 6 g fibre, 120 mg chol, 1,986 mg sodium. % RDI: 7% calcium, 22% iron, 24% vit A, 103% vit C, 37% folate.

Gluten-Free Sweet Potato Pancakes

Look for xanthan gum in health food stores or the health food aisle of some supermarkets. Serve these versatile pancakes with maple syrup and bacon, or omit the cinnamon and serve them with sour cream, chopped chives and smoked salmon.

1½ cups **cornstarch**

1½ cups **white rice flour**

1 tbsp **gluten-free baking powder**

½ tsp **salt**

½ tsp **xanthan gum**

½ tsp **cinnamon**

2 **eggs**

2½ cups **buttermilk**

½ cup **butter,** melted

1 tbsp packed **brown sugar**

1½ cups cooled mashed **cooked sweet potato**
   (1 large sweet potato, about 1 lb/450 g)

3 tbsp **vegetable oil**

In large bowl, whisk together cornstarch, flour, baking powder, salt, xanthan gum and cinnamon.

In separate bowl, beat eggs; whisk in buttermilk, butter and brown sugar. Whisk in sweet potato. Stir into dry ingredients just until combined.

Heat large skillet over medium heat; brush with some of the oil. Spoon ⅓ cup batter per pancake into skillet; cook, turning once, until golden, fluffy and set, about 6 minutes. *(Make-ahead: Let cool. Refrigerate in airtight container for up to 3 days. Reheat in toaster.)*

Makes about 18 pancakes. PER PANCAKE: about 206 cal, 3 g pro, 9 g total fat (4 g sat. fat), 28 g carb, 1 g fibre, 37 mg chol, 197 mg sodium, 147 mg potassium. % RDI: 8% calcium, 4% iron, 49% vit A, 7% vit C, 3% folate.

gluten-free recipes

Pignoli Cookies

These old-fashioned Italian cookies, studded with pine nuts, are crunchy and chewy at the same time. Roll the dough into balls with slightly damp hands to keep it from sticking.

1½ cups **whole blanched almonds**

¾ cup **granulated sugar**

¾ cup **icing sugar**

2 **egg whites**

½ tsp **almond extract**

2 cups **pine nuts** (see Tip, below)

In food processor, coarsely chop almonds. Add granulated sugar and icing sugar; process until in fine crumbs. Add egg whites and almond extract; process for 2 minutes to form smooth sticky dough. Refrigerate for 10 minutes.

Roll by heaping 1 tsp into balls; roll in pine nuts. Place, about 2 inches (5 cm) apart, on parchment paper–lined rimless baking sheets; press to flatten slightly.

Bake in 325°F (160°C) oven until edges are light golden and tops are firm, about 18 minutes. Let cool on pans on racks for 2 minutes. Transfer to racks; let cool. *(Make-ahead: Store in airtight container for up to 5 days.)*

Makes about 36 cookies. PER COOKIE: about 112 cal, 3 g pro, 8 g total fat (1 g sat. fat), 9 g carb, 1 g fibre, 0 mg chol, 5 mg sodium, 89 mg potassium. % RDI: 1% calcium, 4% iron, 2% folate.

best
TIPS
ever

124

Like all nuts, pine nuts and walnuts can go rancid quickly due to their high oil content. For best quality, buy whole nuts or halves and store them in the freezer in an airtight container. Chopped nuts are particularly susceptible to spoilage, so chopping your own is a good idea.

Chocolate Espresso Torte

The centre of this fudgy cake may sink slightly as it cools. If it does, turn it over and top with strawberries and chocolate syrup. If you use potato starch and pareve margarine, the cake is Passover-friendly.

1 cup **walnuts** (see Tip, opposite)

1¼ cups **granulated sugar**

2 tbsp **potato starch** or cornstarch

½ tsp **cinnamon**

¼ tsp **salt**

1 cup **soft margarine** or butter

¼ cup **brewed espresso** or very strong brewed coffee

1 cup **cocoa powder**

4 **eggs,** separated

CHOCOLATE SYRUP:

⅓ cup **cocoa powder**

⅓ cup **liquid honey**

Line bottom and side of 9-inch (2.5 L) springform pan with parchment paper, or grease. Set aside.

In food processor, whirl walnuts with 1 tbsp of the sugar until powdery; whirl in potato starch, cinnamon and salt. Transfer to large bowl; set aside.

In small saucepan, melt margarine with espresso. Whisk in cocoa powder until smooth. Let cool.

Meanwhile, in large bowl, beat egg yolks with ¾ cup of the remaining sugar until thick and pale. Beat in chocolate mixture. Stir into walnut mixture.

In bowl, beat egg whites until soft peaks form. Beat in remaining sugar, 1 tbsp at a time, until stiff glossy peaks form. Fold one-third into chocolate mixture; fold in remaining whites. Scrape into prepared pan; smooth top.

Bake in 350°F (180°C) oven until cake tester inserted in centre comes out clean, about 1¼ hours. Let cool in pan on rack for 10 minutes. Remove side of pan; let cool completely. *(Make-ahead: Cover with plastic wrap and store for up to 1 day.)*

CHOCOLATE SYRUP: In saucepan, bring cocoa powder, honey and ½ cup water to boil; boil until syrupy, about 3 minutes. *(Make-ahead: Let cool. Refrigerate in airtight container for up to 2 days.)* Serve with torte.

Makes 8 to 10 servings. PER EACH OF 10 SERVINGS: about 433 cal, 7 g pro, 30 g total fat (5 g sat. fat), 44 g carb, 4 g fibre, 74 mg chol, 327 mg sodium. % RDI: 4% calcium, 18% iron, 26% vit A, 12% folate.

Vegetable Skewers With Pesto Butter

Grill up these kabobs as a side dish for a vegetarian meal or serve with grilled meat or fish. Either basil pesto or sun-dried tomato pesto will work beautifully in this recipe. No pesto? Add ¼ cup minced fresh basil to the butter.

2 small **zucchini** (10 oz/280 g total)

1 **Japanese eggplant** (6 oz/170 g)

1 each **sweet red pepper** and **sweet yellow pepper**

1 **Cubanelle pepper**

¼ cup **butter,** melted

2 tbsp **pesto**

¼ tsp each **salt** and **pepper**

Cut zucchini and eggplant into ½-inch (1 cm) thick rounds. Core and seed red, yellow and Cubanelle peppers; cut into 1-inch (2.5 cm) pieces.

Onto 8 metal or soaked wooden skewers, alternately thread zucchini, eggplant and peppers. *(Make-ahead: Cover and refrigerate for up to 6 hours.)*

Mix butter with pesto. Sprinkle skewers with salt and pepper; brush with half of the pesto butter. Place on greased grill over medium-high heat; close lid and grill, turning 3 times, until tender, 10 minutes. Brush with remaining pesto butter.

Makes 4 servings. PER SERVING: about 170 cal, 2 g pro, 14 g total fat (8 g sat. fat), 10 g carb, 3 g fibre, 37 mg chol, 354 mg sodium. % RDI: 3% calcium, 6% iron, 26% vit A, 173% vit C, 13% folate.

fresh veggie sides

Purple Chorizo Potatoes

They say your eyes eat before your mouth does – and this dish certainly proves that point. These gorgeous purple potatoes are marvellous as a side dish or served in a big bowl as a potato salad.

3 lb (1.35 kg) **purple potatoes** (about 10 medium), see Tips, below

1 tbsp **vegetable oil**

8 oz (225 g) **dry-cured chorizo** (see Tips, below) or smoked sausage, diced

6 **green onions,** thinly sliced

⅓ cup chopped **oil-cured black olives**

DRESSING:

⅓ cup **white wine vinegar**

1 tbsp **Dijon mustard**

1 clove **garlic,** minced

1 tsp **dried Mexican oregano** or dried regular oregano

½ tsp **salt**

¼ tsp **pepper**

½ cup **vegetable oil**

In Dutch oven, combine potatoes with enough salted water to cover by 1 inch (2.5 cm); bring to boil. Reduce heat and simmer just until tender but not mushy, about 15 minutes. Drain; let cool enough to handle. Cut into bite-size chunks.

Meanwhile, in skillet, heat oil over medium heat; fry chorizo until golden, 3 minutes. Drain on paper towel–lined plate.

DRESSING: In large bowl, whisk vinegar, mustard, garlic, oregano, salt and pepper; gradually whisk in oil until blended.

Add potatoes to dressing; toss to coat. Stir in sausage, green onions and olives; serve at room temperature. *(Make-ahead: Cover and refrigerate for up to 2 days.)*

Makes 8 servings. PER SERVING: about 411 cal, 10 g pro, 28 g total fat (5 g sat. fat), 30 g carb, 3 g fibre, 25 mg chol, 1,026 mg sodium. % RDI: 3% calcium, 15% iron, 1% vit A, 33% vit C, 10% folate.

best **TIPS** ever

- Don't confuse dry-cured chorizo with fresh. Fresh chorizo is uncooked and spiced very differently from the dry-cured variety. Fresh chorizo is delicious grilled on the barbecue or added to recipes that require uncooked sausage. But it doesn't have the dry texture and classic Spanish or Portuguese garlic-paprika spicing that these potatoes cry out for.

- Purple potatoes really soak up the vinaigrette in this recipe, thanks to their high starch content. If you can't find them, use other starchy potatoes, such as new potatoes or fingerlings.

Yellow Tomato Salad With Shallots & Lemongrass

If you can't find lemongrass, substitute 1 tsp grated lemon zest for the stalk.

1 stalk **lemongrass**

¼ cup finely chopped **shallots**

¼ tsp grated **lemon zest**

2 tbsp **lemon juice**

1 clove **garlic,** minced

¼ tsp **salt**

Pinch **cayenne pepper**

6 **yellow tomatoes**

Fresh cilantro leaves

Cut off bottom third of lemongrass; peel off outer layer and slice stalk paper-thin. Whisk together lemongrass, shallots, lemon zest, lemon juice, garlic, salt and cayenne pepper. *(Make-ahead: Cover and refrigerate for up to 24 hours. Whisk before using.)*

Cut each tomato into 8 wedges. Place in large bowl; pour dressing over top and gently toss to coat. Garnish with cilantro leaves.

Makes 4 servings. PER SERVING: about 39 cal, 2 g pro, 1 g total fat (0 g sat. fat), 8 g carb, 2 g fibre, 0 mg chol, 187 mg sodium. % RDI: 2% calcium, 8% iron, 35% vit C, 27% folate.

Cucumber Salad With Fresh Mint

Cucumbers are certainly refreshing on their own, but the lemon-mint dressing here makes them even more enticing.

2 **English cucumbers,** peeled

1½ tsp **salt**

⅓ cup thinly sliced **green onions**

2 tbsp finely chopped **fresh mint**

2 tbsp **lemon juice**

2 tbsp **olive oil**

1 tsp **white wine vinegar**

Halve cucumbers lengthwise; scrape out seeds. Thinly slice.

In colander, sprinkle cucumbers with salt; let stand for 30 minutes. Rinse under cold water and pat dry.

Toss together cucumbers, green onions, mint, lemon juice, oil and vinegar. *(Make-ahead: Refrigerate for up to 8 hours. Serve at room temperature.)*

Makes 8 servings. PER SERVING: about 40 cal, 1 g pro, 4 g total fat (1 g sat. fat), 2 g carb, 1 g fibre, 0 mg chol, 111 mg sodium, 105 mg potassium. % RDI: 1% calcium, 3% iron, 1% vit A, 7% vit C, 6% folate.

rise &
shine

French Toast With Caramelized Bananas & Pecans

French toast is always a hit, but this one is just plain scrumptious. The rum is a decadent optional addition, but it's worth the splurge.

⅓ cup chopped **pecans**

6 **eggs**

1½ cups **5% cream** or milk

2 tbsp **maple syrup**

1 tsp **cinnamon**

1 tsp **vanilla**

¼ tsp **salt**

1 loaf (1 lb/450 g) **egg bread** (challah)

2 tbsp **butter**

CARAMELIZED BANANAS:

2 tbsp **butter**

6 **firm ripe bananas,** halved
   crosswise and lengthwise

¾ cup **maple syrup**

½ cup packed **brown sugar**

¼ cup **corn syrup**

¼ cup **dark rum** (optional)

On baking sheet, toast pecans in 325°F (160°C) oven, about 6 minutes. Set aside.

In large bowl, whisk together eggs, cream, maple syrup, cinnamon, vanilla and salt. Cut egg bread into ¾-inch (2 cm) thick slices; dip into egg mixture until soaked.

In large skillet, melt 1 tbsp of the butter over medium heat; cook slices, in batches and adding more of the remaining butter as needed, until golden, about 3 minutes. Transfer to 2 baking sheets. Bake in top and bottom thirds of 350°F (180°C) oven until puffed and heated through, 8 minutes.

CARAMELIZED BANANAS: Meanwhile, in large nonstick skillet, melt half of the butter over medium-high heat; fry half of the bananas, turning once, until golden and tender, about 3 minutes. Transfer to plate. Repeat with remaining butter and bananas.

In same skillet, bring maple syrup, brown sugar, corn syrup, and rum (if using) to boil over medium-high heat; reduce heat and simmer for 2 minutes. Stir in bananas; simmer for 1 minute. Spoon over French toast; sprinkle with pecans.

Makes 6 to 8 servings. PER EACH OF 8 SERVINGS: about 596 cal, 13 g pro, 19 g total fat (7 g sat. fat), 96 g carb, 3 g fibre, 199 mg chol, 497 mg sodium, 570 mg potassium. % RDI: 17% calcium, 23% iron, 12% vit A, 8% vit C, 34% folate.

Western Omelettes

Omelettes are perfect for families because each member can fill his or her own as desired. Our flavourful variations mean there's a version suited to everyone at the table.

4 tsp **butter**

8 **eggs**

¼ tsp each **salt** and **pepper**

FILLING:

½ cup diced **Black Forest ham** or smoked turkey

½ cup finely chopped **sweet green pepper**

2 **green onions,** chopped

In 8-inch (20 cm) nonstick skillet, melt 1 tsp of the butter over medium heat. In bowl and using fork, beat together 2 of the eggs, 1 tbsp water and pinch each of the salt and pepper; pour into skillet. Cook until eggs are almost set, gently lifting edge with spatula to allow uncooked eggs to flow underneath, about 3 minutes.

FILLING: Sprinkle half of the omelette with 2 tbsp each of the ham and green pepper, and one-quarter of the green onions; fold uncovered half over top and cook for 2 minutes. Slide onto plate.

Repeat with remaining ingredients to make 4 omelettes.

Makes 4 servings. PER SERVING: about 285 cal, 20 g pro, 21 g total fat (10 g sat. fat), 2 g carb, 0 g fibre, 378 mg sodium. % RDI: 29% calcium, 9% iron, 27% vit A, 23% folate.

change it up

Spinach & Smoked Sausage Omelettes: Omit Filling. Fill omelettes with 1⅓ cups lightly packed shredded fresh baby spinach; ½ cup diced smoked sausage; and 2 cloves garlic, minced.

Tomato & Goat Cheese Omelettes: Omit Filling. Fill omelettes with 1 cup diced plum tomatoes; ⅓ cup soft goat cheese; and 2 green onions, thinly sliced.

Egg White Omelettes: Omit eggs and water. Use 12 egg whites. Omit Filling. Fill omelettes with 1 cup shredded light cheese (such as Danbo or Havarti) and 2 tbsp finely chopped fresh herbs (such as parsley, chives, oregano or basil). For each omelette, use 3 egg whites and cook as directed.

best **TIPS** ever

A good nonstick omelette pan is a smart investment. Look for one that is nicely balanced and sits flat on the burner. Some smaller pans can be overwhelmed by too-heavy handles (which make them tip over), so test the pan on a flat surface before you buy.

Shredded Hash Browns

Everyone loves these lacy fried shredded potatoes. Here, they cook in a single, easy-to-make cake that you can cut into wedges. Serve with ketchup, sour cream or applesauce – whichever you prefer.

4 **baking potatoes** (about 2 lb/900 g total), peeled

¼ cup **butter**

1 large **onion,** thinly sliced

½ tsp **salt**

¼ tsp **pepper**

¼ cup **whipping cream (35%)**

In saucepan of boiling salted water, cook potatoes until slightly softened, about 10 minutes. Drain and refrigerate until cold, about 2 hours. *(Make-ahead: Refrigerate for up to 24 hours.)*

Coarsely shred potatoes; set aside. In extra-large nonstick skillet, melt butter over medium heat; fry onion until softened, about 5 minutes. Stir in potatoes, salt and pepper; cook, stirring a few times, until crisp and golden, about 12 minutes.

Drizzle in cream; cook until absorbed, 2 minutes. Remove from heat; let stand for 1 hour. *(Make-ahead: Let stand for up to 3 hours.)*

Fry over medium heat, turning a few times, until crispy and browned, about 2 minutes. Cut into wedges.

Makes 6 servings. PER SERVING: about 215 cal, 3 g pro, 11 g total fat (7 g sat. fat), 27 g carb, 2 g fibre, 33 mg chol, 540 mg sodium, 444 mg potassium. % RDI: 2% calcium, 4% iron, 10% vit A, 15% vit C, 7% folate.

Tomato Potato Galette

Serve this show-off tart as a vegetarian main dish or as a side dish. This is a great pastry for beginners to try, since the free-form look of a galette is very relaxed and forgiving.

1½ cups **all-purpose flour**

¼ tsp **salt**

Pinch **cayenne pepper**

⅓ cup each cold **butter** and **shortening**

1 tsp **vinegar**

¼ cup **cold water** (approx)

FILLING:

3 **yellow-fleshed potatoes** (1¼ lb/ 565 g total), peeled

6 **plum tomatoes**

1 tsp **salt**

½ tsp **pepper**

1 tbsp **extra-virgin olive oil**

2 **onions,** sliced

2 cloves **garlic,** minced

½ tsp **dried rosemary,** crumbled (or crushed aniseed)

1½ cups shredded **Asiago cheese**

2 **eggs,** beaten

1 tbsp grated **Parmesan cheese**

In bowl, stir together flour, salt and cayenne pepper. With pastry blender or 2 knives, cut in butter and shortening until in fine crumbs with a few larger pieces. Stirring with fork, pour in vinegar and enough of the water to make soft ragged dough. Press into disc; wrap in plastic wrap and refrigerate until chilled, about 30 minutes.

FILLING: In large saucepan of boiling salted water, cover and cook potatoes just until tender, about 20 minutes. Drain and let cool. Thinly slice crosswise; transfer to large bowl.

Meanwhile, cut tomatoes lengthwise into ½-inch (1 cm) thick slices; place on foil-lined baking sheet. Sprinkle with pinch each of the salt and pepper; broil, turning once, until slightly shrivelled and edges are blackened, 10 minutes. Let cool.

Meanwhile, in skillet, heat oil over medium heat; cook onions, garlic, rosemary and remaining salt and pepper, stirring occasionally, until onions are golden, about 10 minutes. Add to potatoes along with Asiago cheese and all but 1 tbsp of the eggs; toss gently to combine.

On floured surface, roll out pastry into 16-inch (40 cm) circle; place on pizza pan. Leaving 2-inch (5 cm) border uncovered, spread potato mixture over pastry. Arrange tomatoes over top; sprinkle with Parmesan cheese. Fold border over top, pleating to fit. Brush pastry with remaining eggs.

Bake on bottom rack in 400°F (200°C) oven until golden, 40 to 45 minutes. Let cool in pan on rack for 10 minutes before cutting into wedges. *(Make-ahead: Let cool. Cover and refrigerate for up to 6 hours. Reheat before serving.)*

Makes 6 servings. PER SERVING: about 544 cal, 14 g pro, 34 g total fat (16 g sat. fat), 46 g carb, 3 g fibre, 1,031 mg sodium. % RDI: 24% calcium, 16% iron, 25% vit A, 27% vit C, 25% folate.

hearty sunday brunch

Herbed Turkey Sausage Patties

Why buy premade sausage when you can make this ultra-savoury recipe at home? The patties are a lighter but still delicious alternative to bacon or breakfast sausages.

6 oz (170 g) **pancetta,** skinned and diced (see Tip, below)

1¼ lb (565 g) **lean ground turkey**

¼ cup finely diced **shallots** or red onions

1 **egg**

1 tbsp finely chopped **fresh sage** or fresh parsley

1 tbsp **Dijon mustard**

½ tsp each **pepper** and **sweet paprika**

¼ tsp **salt**

1 tbsp **vegetable oil** or olive oil

In food processor, pulse pancetta until coarsely ground; transfer to bowl. Add turkey, shallots, egg, sage, mustard, pepper, paprika and salt to bowl; mix with hands. Shape by ¼ cup into patties.

In large skillet, heat half of the oil over medium-high heat. In 2 batches and adding remaining oil as necessary, fry patties, turning once, until instant-read thermometer inserted sideways into several reads 165°F (74°C), about 8 minutes.

Makes 6 servings. PER SERVING: about 226 cal, 21 g pro, 15 g total fat (4 g sat. fat), 2 g carb, trace fibre, 101 mg chol, 388 mg sodium, 252 mg potassium. % RDI: 3% calcium, 11% iron, 3% vit A, 5% folate.

best **TIPS** ever

Pancetta is easier to dice when it's partially frozen. Pull the skin off, then place the pancetta on a plate and freeze until firm, about 30 minutes.

Pink Grapefruit Mimosa These variations on the traditional mimosa made of orange juice and bubbly – the consummate brunch cocktail – are fruity, fun ways to start the meal.

2 oz (¼ cup) **pink grapefruit juice**

3 oz (6 tbsp) **dry white sparkling wine** or Champagne

Pour pink grapefruit juice into champagne flute; top with sparkling wine.

Makes 1 serving. PER SERVING: about 92 cal, trace pro, 0 g total fat (0 g sat. fat), 9 g carb, 0 g fibre, 0 mg chol, 5 mg sodium. % RDI: 1% calcium, 3% iron, 37% vit C.

change it up

Passion Fruit Mimosa: Substitute passion fruit juice for the pink grapefruit juice.

Cranberry Mimosa: Substitute cranberry juice for the pink grapefruit juice.

Strata-touille
This colourful vegetable, egg and cheese dish deliciously echoes the flavours of ratatouille. The best part is that you can make the casserole portion a day ahead, then bake it with the tomato topping at the last minute.

2 tbsp **extra-virgin olive oil**

2 cloves **garlic,** minced

1 tbsp chopped **fresh oregano**
  (or 2 tsp dried)

½ tsp each **salt** and **pepper**

3 **zucchini,** thinly sliced

5 **sweet peppers** (green,
  red and/or yellow)

6 **eggs**

1½ cups **milk**

1 cup **10% cream**

1 tsp **dry mustard**

Dash **hot pepper sauce**

24 slices **egg bread** (challah), about 1 loaf

1½ cups each shredded **Asiago cheese** and
  mozzarella cheese

2 tbsp chopped **fresh parsley**

OVEN-ROASTED TOMATOES:

4 cups **cherry tomatoes**

1 tbsp **extra-virgin olive oil**

2 tsp chopped **fresh rosemary** (or 1 tsp dried)

1 clove **garlic,** minced

Pinch each **salt** and **pepper**

In bowl, combine oil, garlic, 1 tsp of the oregano and ¼ tsp each of the salt and pepper. Add zucchini; toss to coat. Reserving oil mixture, arrange zucchini on foil-lined rimmed baking sheet; broil until tender and browned, 6 minutes.

Core, seed and cut sweet peppers into quarters. Spread on foil-lined rimmed baking sheet; broil, turning once, until skins are loose and blackened, 10 minutes. Let cool enough to handle; peel off skins. Toss peppers with reserved oil mixture.

In large dish, whisk eggs, milk, cream, mustard, hot pepper sauce and remaining oregano, salt and pepper; set aside.

Trim crusts from bread; cut slices diagonally in half. Dip into egg mixture, turning to soak well. Arrange 16 bread triangles in greased 13- x 9-inch (3 L) baking dish; sprinkle with one-third each of the Asiago and mozzarella cheeses. Cover with zucchini. Repeat bread and cheese layers once.

Cover with sweet peppers, alternating colours. Top with remaining egg-soaked bread; pour remaining egg mixture over top. Sprinkle with parsley and remaining cheese. Cover with plastic wrap; place another baking dish or plates over surface. Refrigerate for 4 hours. *(Make-ahead: Refrigerate for up to 24 hours.)* Uncover and bake in 375°F (190°C) oven until crusty and golden, about 1 hour.

OVEN-ROASTED TOMATOES: Meanwhile, in small baking dish, toss tomatoes, oil, rosemary, garlic, salt and pepper. Bake in 375°F (190°C) oven until soft and juicy, 1 hour. Serve on strata.

Makes 16 servings. PER SERVING: about 314 cal, 14 g pro, 15 g total fat (6 g sat. fat), 31 g carb, 3 g fibre, 119 mg chol, 488 mg sodium. % RDI: 23% calcium, 16% iron, 20% vit A, 90% vit C, 30% folate.

make-ahead breakfasts

Fruity Breakfast Crisp

Sure, crisps are usually served for dessert. But they can also be a healthy breakfast! Make and refrigerate this one the night before and warm it in the oven as you're getting ready for work or school.

4 cups sliced peeled **peaches**
  (see Tips, below)

4 cups quartered **plums**

2 tbsp **all-purpose flour**

2 tbsp **granulated sugar**

¾ cup **whole wheat flour**

¾ cup **large-flake rolled oats**

½ cup packed **brown sugar**

¼ cup **unsalted hulled sunflower seeds**

3 tbsp **wheat germ** (see Tips, below)

⅓ cup **butter,** melted

1 tbsp **apple juice**

Toss together peaches, plums, all-purpose flour and granulated sugar; arrange in 8-inch (2 L) square baking dish.

In bowl, combine whole wheat flour, oats, brown sugar, sunflower seeds and wheat germ; stir in butter and apple juice. Sprinkle over fruit mixture.

Bake in 375°F (190°C) oven until bubbly and golden, 45 to 55 minutes. Let cool for 30 minutes. *(Make-ahead: Cover and refrigerate for up to 1 day.)* Serve warm or at room temperature.

Makes 8 servings. PER SERVING: about 329 cal, 6 g pro, 12 g total fat (5 g sat. fat), 55 g carb, 6 g fibre, 20 mg chol, 60 mg sodium, 435 mg potassium. % RDI: 3% calcium, 12% iron, 12% vit A, 17% vit C, 12% folate.

best
TIPS
ever

- This recipe works just as well with unpeeled nectarines as it does with peaches.

- Wheat germ is high in vitamin E, a powerful antioxidant. It's excellent in baked goods, sprinkled over oatmeal and even stirred into yogurt or smoothies.

Cheddar Bacon Muffins

For people who prefer savoury to sweet, these hearty muffins are an ideal – and quick! – meal. They're pretty rich on their own, but we won't tell if you top one with a little pat of butter.

6 slices **bacon**

1 cup shredded **old Cheddar cheese**

3 cups **all-purpose flour**

2 tbsp **granulated sugar**

4 tsp **baking powder**

2 tsp **pepper**

1 tsp **salt**

1 cup **milk**

½ cup **vegetable oil**

½ cup sliced **green onions**

½ cup **sour cream**

2 **eggs**

In skillet, cook bacon over medium heat until crisp, about 5 minutes. Let cool on paper towel–lined plate; crumble. Stir 1 tbsp of the crumbled bacon with 2 tbsp of the Cheddar cheese; set aside.

In large bowl, whisk together flour, sugar, baking powder, pepper and salt; stir in remaining bacon and cheese.

Whisk together milk, oil, green onions, sour cream and eggs; pour over dry ingredients. Stir just until moistened. Spoon into greased or paper-lined muffin cups; sprinkle reserved bacon mixture over tops.

Bake in 375°F (190°C) oven until golden and tops are firm to the touch, 20 to 25 minutes. *(Make-ahead: Refrigerate in airtight container for up to 1 day or wrap individually and freeze in airtight container for up to 3 weeks. Reheat to serve.)*

Makes 12 servings. PER SERVING: about 301 cal, 10 g pro, 17 g total fat (4 g sat. fat), 27 g carb, 1 g fibre, 49 mg chol, 451 mg sodium, 135 mg potassium. % RDI: 15% calcium, 14% iron, 7% vit A, 2% vit C, 25% folate.

Sweet Potato Pancakes

Hash browns and latkes are high on so many people's list of favourites. Why not give these crispy potato pancakes a nutrient (and flavour) boost by adding sweet potatoes?

2 **russet potatoes** (1½ lb/675 g total)

1 **sweet potato** (12 oz/340 g)

3 **eggs**

1 tsp **Cajun seasoning**

¼ tsp each **salt** and **pepper**

2 tbsp **butter**

2 tbsp **vegetable oil**

Peel russet and sweet potatoes. By hand or in food processor using shredder blade, grate russet and sweet potatoes; squeeze out liquid. In large bowl, whisk together eggs, Cajun seasoning, salt and pepper; add potatoes and toss to coat.

In large skillet, heat one-quarter each of the butter and oil over medium-low heat. Drop potato mixture by ¼ cupfuls into skillet; press to flatten slightly. Fry, in batches, turning once and adding remaining butter and oil as necessary, until tender and edges are golden, about 15 minutes. *(Make-ahead: Refrigerate in airtight container for up to 24 hours. Reheat on baking sheet in 450°F/230°C oven until crisp and hot in centre, about 5 minutes.)*

Makes 8 servings. PER SERVING: about 170 cal, 4 g pro, 8 g total fat (3 g sat. fat), 21 g carb, 2 g fibre, 77 mg chol, 141 mg sodium. % RDI: 2% calcium, 6% iron, 65% vit A, 17% vit C, 8% folate.

easy weekend brunch

Stuffed Baked Tomatoes & Eggs With Pancetta

Plump, juicy heirloom tomatoes make tasty cups for pesto, pancetta and soft-cooked egg.

8 **heirloom tomatoes** or vine-ripened tomatoes (2½-inch/6 cm diameter)

½ tsp **salt**

3 tbsp **basil pesto**

8 thin slices **pancetta** (at least 3-inch/8 cm diameter) or thinly sliced prosciutto (see Tip, below)

8 small **eggs,** at room temperature

4 tsp **butter**

Grease 8 mini-muffin or shallow muffin cups; place on rimmed baking sheet. Set aside.

Cut top off each tomato to make 1½-inch (4 cm) wide hole. With spoon, gently scrape out pulp and seeds. Sprinkle insides with salt; place, cut side down, on paper towel–lined plate. Let stand for 30 minutes.

Place tomatoes, cut side up, in prepared muffin cups to secure (tomatoes do not need to fit inside cups). Using paper towel, lightly blot insides to remove any moisture. *(Make-ahead: Cover and refrigerate for up to 12 hours; bring to room temperature to continue.)*

Spoon pesto into tomatoes. Line inside of each with slice of pancetta, pressing down and along side to create cup for egg. Crack egg into each tomato cup; dot with butter. Bake in 400°F (200°C) oven until whites are set and yolks are still runny, 18 to 22 minutes.

Makes 4 servings. PER SERVING: about 413 cal, 16 g pro, 34 g total fat (16 g sat. fat), 11 g carb, 3 g fibre, 314 mg chol, 808 mg sodium. % RDI: 8% calcium, 13% iron, 34% vit A, 47% vit C, 28% folate.

Radicchio & Pear Salad

Ripe pears and a honey mustard vinaigrette give these peppery greens a sweet, fruity edge that complements savoury baked eggs.

1 head **radicchio,** cored

1 bunch **arugula,** trimmed

1 head **Belgian endive,** trimmed

2 **pears,** chopped

DRESSING:

¼ cup **vegetable oil**

3 tbsp **cider vinegar**

2 tbsp **liquid honey**

1 tbsp **Dijon mustard**

¼ tsp **salt**

¼ tsp **pepper**

DRESSING: Whisk together oil, vinegar, honey, mustard, salt and pepper.

Tear radicchio and arugula into bite-size pieces; add to large bowl. Halve endive lengthwise; slice crosswise and add to bowl. *(Make-ahead: Cover with damp paper towel; refrigerate for up to 4 hours.)*

Sprinkle pears over greens. Add dressing; toss to coat.

Makes 8 servings. PER SERVING: about 114 cal, 1 g pro, 7 g total fat (1 g sat. fat), 13 g carb, 2 g fibre, 0 mg chol, 107 mg sodium. % RDI: 4% calcium, 4% iron, 4% vit A, 12% vit C, 19% folate.

best **TIPS** ever

Pancetta is unsmoked cured pork belly – the same cut that goes into regular smoked bacon. Pancetta must be cooked, just like bacon. In this recipe, you can substitute prosciutto if you like. Prosciutto is cut from the leg, rather than the belly, so it will give the dish a slightly meatier flavour.

Vanilla Latte

Caffe latte is one-third espresso and two-thirds steamed milk, making it milder and milkier than cappuccino. Sweetened with vanilla syrup, it's perfect for brunch.

1 cup **brewed espresso** or double-
   strength coffee
¼ cup **Vanilla Syrup** (right)
2 cups **hot milk** or steamed milk
½ cup **whipped cream** or
   frothed milk
Vanilla sugar and **nutmeg** (optional)

Pour ¼ cup espresso into each of 4 coffee cups or mugs. Stir 1 tbsp vanilla syrup into each; add ½ cup hot milk. Top with whipped cream; sprinkle with vanilla sugar and nutmeg (if using).

Makes 4 servings. PER SERVING: about 160 cal, 4 g pro, 8 g total fat (4 g sat. fat), 19 g carb, 0 g fibre, 29 mg chol, 72 mg sodium. 252 mg potassium. % RDI: 14% calcium, 1% iron, 13% vit A, 3% folate.

Vanilla Syrup

This simple syrup adds sweetness and just a touch of vanilla's heavenly perfume to a cup of tea or coffee. Keep a jar in the fridge to enjoy in your daily cuppa.

1 cup **granulated sugar**
1 tsp **vanilla**

In saucepan, bring sugar and 1 cup water to boil; reduce heat and simmer until syrupy, about 5 minutes.

Add vanilla; transfer to jar. *(Make-ahead: Seal and refrigerate for up to 2 weeks.)*

Makes 1 cup. PER 1 TBSP: about 49 cal, 0 g pro, 0 g total fat (0 g sat. fat), 13 g carb, 0 g fibre, 0 mg chol, 1 mg sodium, 0 mg potassium.

Lemon Ricotta Pancakes With Berry Compote

Loaded with sweet blueberries and topped with a mixed berry compote, there's no need to add calorie-laden butter or syrup to these pancakes. Wild blueberries have the best flavour, but you can use cultivated berries when wild aren't in season.

1½ cups **all-purpose flour**

1 tbsp **granulated sugar**

1 tbsp **baking powder**

½ tsp **salt**

½ cup **extra-smooth ricotta cheese**

1 **egg**

1½ cups **milk**

¼ cup **butter,** melted

2 tsp grated **lemon zest**

1 cup **fresh blueberries**

Vegetable oil

BERRY COMPOTE:

1 cup sliced **fresh strawberries**

½ cup **fresh blueberries**

½ cup **fresh raspberries**

2 tbsp **granulated sugar**

1 tbsp **lemon juice**

BERRY COMPOTE: In bowl, combine strawberries, blueberries, raspberries, sugar and lemon juice. Set aside.

In large bowl, whisk together flour, sugar, baking powder and salt.

Press ricotta through fine-mesh sieve into separate bowl. Whisk in egg, milk, butter and lemon zest. Pour over dry ingredients, stirring just until moistened. Fold in blueberries.

Brush large nonstick skillet with oil; heat over medium heat. Using ¼ cup batter per pancake, pour in batter, spreading to form 5-inch (12 cm) circles.

Cook until bubbles break on tops but do not fill in, about 1½ minutes. Turn and cook until bottoms are golden, 1 to 2 minutes. Serve with berry compote.

Makes 4 servings. PER SERVING: about 479 cal, 13 g pro, 19 g total fat (9 g sat. fat), 66 g carb, 5 g fibre, 84 mg chol, 650 mg sodium, 353 mg potassium. % RDI: 22% calcium, 21% iron, 16% vit A, 60% vit C, 55% folate.

pancake breakfast

Chocolate Chip Pancakes

What breakfast is guaranteed to make you feel like a kid again? These chocolaty wonders! The optional chocolate syrup and whipped cream make the pancakes a creative option for dessert too.

1½ cups **all-purpose flour**

1 tbsp **granulated sugar**

1 tbsp **baking powder**

½ tsp **salt**

1 **egg**

1½ cups **milk**

¼ cup **butter,** melted, or vegetable oil

½ cup **chocolate chips**

Vegetable oil

Chocolate syrup and whipped cream (optional)

In large bowl, whisk together flour, sugar, baking powder and salt. Whisk egg, milk and butter; stir into dry ingredients just until lumpy. Stir in chocolate chips just until incorporated.

Brush large nonstick skillet with oil; heat over medium heat. Using ¼ cup batter for each pancake, pour in batter, spreading with spatula if necessary.

Cook until bubbles break on tops but do not fill in, about 2 minutes. Turn and cook until bottoms are golden, 1 to 2 minutes. Serve topped with chocolate syrup and whipped cream (if using).

Makes 14 pancakes. PER PANCAKE: about 267 cal, 3 g pro, 22 g total fat (5 g sat. fat), 16 g carb, 1 g fibre, 24 mg chol, 187 mg sodium, 79 mg potassium. % RDI: 6% calcium, 6% iron, 5% vit A, 10% folate.

Big Batch Scrambled Eggs

For a large group, these eggs are an easy answer. If you don't have a big enough skillet, use two or cook them in two batches.

4 cups **eggs** (about 20)
1 cup **milk** or water
½ tsp **salt**
Pinch **pepper**
2 tbsp **butter** or vegetable oil

In large bowl, beat together eggs, milk, salt and pepper.

In deep 12-inch (30 cm) skillet or shallow Dutch oven, melt butter over medium-high heat; pour in egg mixture and reduce heat to medium-low. Cook until beginning to set. Gently draw spatula across bottom of pan to form large soft curds; cook until thickened and moist but no visible liquid remains, 20 to 25 minutes. Serve immediately or keep warm over pan of hot water.

Makes 10 servings. PER SERVING: about 181 cal, 13 g pro, 13 g total fat (5 g sat. fat), 2 g carb, 0 g fibre, 276 mg sodium. % RDI: 7% calcium, 11% iron, 22% vit A, 16% folate.

Tropical Fruit Salad

This bright, sweet brunch starter works well with all sorts of combos. Try it with a mix of mango, melon, lichee, papaya, pineapple and/or star fruit.

2 tbsp **liquid honey**
2 tbsp **orange juice** or grapefruit juice
4 cups chopped peeled **fresh tropical fruit**
1 tbsp shredded **fresh mint**
¼ cup **pomegranate seeds**

In large bowl, stir honey with orange juice. Add fruit and mint; toss to coat. Garnish with pomegranate seeds. *(Make-ahead: Cover and refrigerate for up to 8 hours.)*

Makes 4 servings. PER SERVING: about 118 cal, 1 g pro, trace total fat (0 g sat. fat), 30 g carb, 2 g fibre, 0 mg chol, 6 mg sodium. % RDI: 2% calcium, 4% iron, 16% vit A, 102% vit C, 7% folate.

best **TIPS** ever

When you're using a large number of eggs for a single recipe, as in these crowd-worthy scrambled eggs (above), crack each one into a smaller bowl first. Check the quality of the egg and pick out any stray bits of shell before you add it to the others. There's nothing worse than adding a bad egg at the end and ruining the whole batch.

Poppy Seed Bagels

The satisfying chewy texture of these homemade bagels makes them ideal for breakfast on the run, a quick lunch or a snack any time of day. They're good with sandwich fillings – and great for perking up a lunch box.

2 tbsp + 1 tsp **granulated sugar**

⅔ cup lukewarm **potato water**
   (see Tips, page 154)

1 pkg (8 g) **active dry yeast** (1 tbsp)

2 **eggs**

3 tbsp **vegetable oil**

3 cups **all-purpose flour** (approx)

1½ tsp **salt**

POACHING LIQUID:

2 tbsp **granulated sugar**

GLAZE:

1 **egg yolk**

Poppy seeds or sesame seeds

In large bowl, dissolve 1 tsp of the sugar in potato water. Sprinkle in yeast; let stand until frothy, about 10 minutes.

Stir eggs and oil into yeast mixture. Whisk together 1 cup of the flour, the remaining 2 tbsp sugar and salt. Using electric mixer, gradually beat into yeast mixture; beat until smooth, about 2 minutes.

With wooden spoon, gradually stir in enough of the remaining flour to make soft sticky dough.

Turn dough out onto lightly floured surface; knead until smooth and elastic, 5 to 10 minutes. Place in greased bowl, turning to grease all over. Cover and let rise until doubled in bulk, 1 to 1½ hours.

Punch down dough; knead several times. Divide into 12 equal portions; shape each into ball. Keeping remainder covered, twirl 1 ball at a time around finger to form ring. Place on floured baking sheet; cover and let rise for 15 minutes.

POACHING LIQUID: Meanwhile, in Dutch oven, bring 16 cups water to boil; add sugar. Slip bagels into water, 4 to 6 at a time; cook over medium heat for 1 minute. Turn; cook for 1 minute. Using slotted spoon, transfer bagels to parchment paper–lined baking sheet.

GLAZE: Stir egg yolk with 1 tbsp water; brush over bagels. Sprinkle with poppy seeds. Bake in 400°F (200°C) oven until tops are golden and bottoms sound hollow when tapped, 20 to 25 minutes. Let cool on rack.

Makes 12 bagels. PER BAGEL: about 183 cal, 6 g pro, 6 g total fat (1 g sat. fat), 26 g carb, 1 g fibre, 47 mg chol, 299 mg sodium, 75 mg potassium. % RDI: 3% calcium, 14% iron, 2% vit A, 31% folate.

bagels for brunch

Gin Tarragon Gravlax

This Scandinavian specialty is easy to make, but it does take time – the five days of curing is what gives the fish its distinctive flavour and texture. Serve thin slices with bagels, or wrap around breadsticks for a pretty appetizer.

⅓ cup **granulated sugar**

¼ cup **kosher salt** or pickling salt

1 tsp **black peppercorns,** crushed
(see Tips, below)

1 tsp **coriander seeds,** coarsely ground

1 **shallot,** finely diced

3 tbsp chopped **fresh tarragon**

2 lb (900 g) **skin-on centre-cut salmon fillet**

2 tbsp **gin**

In bowl, combine sugar, salt, peppercorns and coriander seeds; mix in shallot and tarragon. Place one-third down centre of sheet of plastic wrap; place salmon, skin side down, on spice mix. Spread remaining spice mix all over flesh side of salmon; drizzle with gin. Wrap in plastic wrap.

Transfer to small baking sheet. Place small cutting board on salmon; weigh down with 2 or 3 full 28-oz (796 mL) cans. Refrigerate for 5 days, turning daily.

Unwrap fish. Using paper towel, brush off most of the spice mix. Thinly slice salmon at 45-degree angle.

Makes about 50 pieces. PER PIECE: about 39 cal, 4 g pro, 2 g total fat (trace sat. fat), 1 g carb, 0 g fibre, 11 mg chol, 367 mg sodium, 68 mg potassium. % RDI: 1% iron, 2% vit C, 2% folate.

best **TIPS** ever

• To make potato water for Poppy Seed Bagels (page 153), save the cooking liquid used to boil potatoes. Cover and refrigerate for up to 3 days or freeze for up to 4 months. (Or dissolve 1 tbsp potato flour in ⅔ cup lukewarm water.)

• A mortar and pestle is good for reducing the peppercorns and coriander seeds to a coarse, not powdery, consistency for the Gin Tarragon Gravlax (above). If you don't have one, use the bottom of a heavy skillet or the flat side of a meat mallet to press (without pounding) on the spices.

Sun-Dried Tomato, Cheese & Basil Pâté

This special-occasion spread is light on calories but heavy on taste. Press it into a pretty serving bowl and surround with fresh bagels. For a party, serve with lots of crisp cracker bread or toasted baguette slices.

12 **dry-packed sun-dried tomatoes**

1 pkg (250 g) **light cream cheese,** softened

½ cup chopped **fresh parsley**

¼ cup chopped **fresh basil**

1 clove **garlic,** minced

2 tbsp **light sour cream**

1 tbsp **extra-virgin olive oil**

Pinch each **salt** and **pepper**

In bowl, cover sun-dried tomatoes with boiling water; let stand for 10 minutes. Drain and finely chop.

Blend together tomatoes, cream cheese, parsley, basil, garlic, sour cream, oil, salt and pepper. *(Make-ahead: Place plastic wrap directly on surface and refrigerate for up to 24 hours.)*

Makes 1½ cups. PER 1 TBSP: about 35 cal, 1 g pro, 3 g total fat (1 g sat. fat), 1 g carb, trace fibre, 9 mg chol, 70 mg sodium. % RDI: 2% calcium, 1% iron, 1% vit A, 3% vit C, 2% folate.

Blueberry Oatmeal Squares

Coffee shops usually have lovely bars and squares, but there's no need to go out for them when you can bake these at home. Oats and blueberries make this an addictive morning treat or dessert.

2½ cups **rolled oats** (not instant)

1¼ cups **all-purpose flour**

1 cup packed **brown sugar**

1 tbsp grated **orange zest**

¼ tsp **salt**

1 cup cold **butter,** cubed

FILLING:

3 cups **fresh blueberries**

½ cup **granulated sugar**

⅓ cup **orange juice**

4 tsp **cornstarch**

FILLING: In saucepan, bring blueberries, sugar and orange juice to boil; reduce heat and simmer until tender, about 10 minutes. Whisk cornstarch with 2 tbsp water; whisk into blueberry mixture and boil, stirring, until thickened, about 1 minute. Place plastic wrap directly on surface; refrigerate until cooled, about 1 hour.

In large bowl, whisk together oats, flour, brown sugar, orange zest and salt; with pastry blender or 2 knives, cut in butter until in coarse crumbs. Press half into parchment paper–lined 8-inch (2 L) square cake pan; spread with blueberry filling. Sprinkle with remaining oat mixture, pressing lightly.

Bake in 350°F (180°C) oven until light golden, 45 minutes. Let cool in pan on rack before cutting into squares. *(Make-ahead: Cover and refrigerate for up to 2 days or overwrap with heavy-duty foil and freeze for up to 2 weeks.)*

Makes 24 squares. PER SQUARE: about 193 cal, 2 g pro, 8 g total fat (5 g sat. fat), 28 g carb, 2 g fibre, 20 mg chol, 84 mg sodium. % RDI: 2% calcium, 7% iron, 7% vit A, 5% vit C, 8% folate.

Cranberry Flax Muffins

Dotted with tangy cranberries and full of healthy fibre, these muffins are a tasty, smart way to start the day.

1 cup **flaxseeds** (see Tip, below)

1 cup **all-purpose flour**

1 cup **whole wheat flour**

1 cup **natural bran**

1 tbsp **baking powder**

1 tsp each **baking soda** and **cinnamon**

½ tsp **salt**

2 **eggs**

1½ cups **buttermilk**

1 cup packed **brown sugar**

⅓ cup **vegetable oil**

1½ cups **dried cranberries**

Set aside 2 tbsp of the flaxseeds. In food processor, finely grind remaining flaxseeds; transfer to large bowl. Add all-purpose flour, whole wheat flour, natural bran, baking powder, baking soda, cinnamon and salt; whisk to combine.

Whisk together eggs, buttermilk, brown sugar and oil; pour over dry ingredients. Sprinkle with cranberries; stir just until combined.

Spoon into 12 greased or paper-lined muffin cups; sprinkle with reserved flaxseeds. Bake in 375°F (190°C) oven until tops are firm to the touch, 20 minutes. Let cool in pan on rack for 5 minutes; transfer to rack and let cool completely.

Makes 12 muffins. PER MUFFIN: about 338 cal, 8 g pro, 12 g total fat (1 g sat. fat), 54 g carb, 7 g fibre, 32 mg chol, 315 mg sodium. % RDI: 12% calcium, 25% iron, 2% vit A, 5% vit C, 29% folate.

best **TIPS** ever

Flaxseeds are another baking staple that can go rancid at room temperature – especially when you buy them already ground. Keep a jar of whole seeds in the freezer and grind just the amount you need at one time.

Lemon Poppy Seed Loaf This ever-popular loaf has a tangy lemon syrup that seeps addictively into the cake, keeping it moist and tender.

½ cup **butter,** softened

1 cup **granulated sugar**

2 **eggs**

1½ cups **all-purpose flour**

3 tbsp **poppy seeds**

1 tbsp grated **lemon zest**

1 tsp **baking powder**

¼ tsp **salt**

½ cup **milk**

LEMON SYRUP:

⅓ cup **granulated sugar**

1 tsp grated **lemon zest**

⅓ cup **lemon juice**

In large bowl, beat butter with sugar until light and fluffy; beat in eggs, 1 at a time, beating well after each addition.

Whisk together flour, poppy seeds, lemon zest, baking powder and salt; stir into butter mixture alternately with milk, making 3 additions of flour mixture and 2 of milk. Spread in greased 8- x 4-inch (1.5 L) loaf pan.

Bake in 325°F (160°C) oven until cake tester inserted in centre comes out clean, about 1 hour. Place pan on rack.

LEMON SYRUP: In saucepan or microwaveable glass measure, warm together sugar, lemon zest and lemon juice until sugar is dissolved. With skewer, pierce hot loaf in 12 places right to bottom; pour lemon syrup over loaf.

Let cool in pan for 30 minutes; turn out onto rack and let cool completely. Wrap and let stand for 12 hours before slicing. *(Make-ahead: Store at room temperature for up to 2 days or overwrap with heavy-duty foil and freeze for up to 2 weeks.)*

Makes 1 loaf, 12 slices. PER SLICE: about 241 cal, 3 g pro, 10 g total fat (5 g sat. fat), 36 g carb, 1 g fibre, 52 mg chol, 164 mg sodium. % RDI: 6% calcium, 7% iron, 9% vit A, 5% vit C, 10% folate.

Individual Brandied Apricot Galettes

If the dried apricots for these luscious mini pies are especially moist, you may have brandy left in the bowl after microwaving. If so, strain and reserve it to add to your coffee.

¾ cup **dried apricots,** thinly sliced

¼ cup **brandy**

½ cup **cream cheese,** softened

¼ cup **granulated sugar**

1 **egg yolk**

½ tsp **vanilla**

1 **egg**

1 pkg (450 g) **frozen butter puff pastry,** thawed and unrolled

¼ cup **apricot jam**

¼ cup chopped **pistachios**

In microwaveable bowl, microwave apricots with brandy on high for 30 seconds; let stand for 10 minutes.

In separate bowl, beat together cream cheese, sugar, egg yolk and vanilla until smooth; set aside. Beat egg with 2 tsp water for egg wash; set aside.

On lightly floured surface and working with 1 sheet of pastry at a time, cut out 4 rounds using 4½-inch (11 cm) round cutter. Leaving ½-inch (1 cm) border, spread each round with about 1 tsp apricot jam. Spread with some of the cream cheese mixture; top with some of the apricots and pistachios.

Brush border with some of the egg wash; fold up border to make ½-inch (1 cm) thick rim, pinching or folding as needed. Transfer to parchment paper–lined rimmed baking sheets; brush edge with remaining egg wash. Refrigerate for 30 minutes. *(Make-ahead: Freeze on baking sheets until firm, then layer between waxed paper in airtight container and freeze for up to 2 weeks. Bake from frozen, adding 3 to 4 minutes to baking time.)*

Bake, 1 sheet at a time, in 425°F (220°C) oven, until puffed and golden, 15 to 18 minutes.

Makes 8 servings. PER SERVING: about 330 cal, 5 g pro, 17 g total fat (8 g sat. fat), 36 g carb, 2 g fibre, 79 mg chol, 170 mg sodium, 215 mg potassium. % RDI: 3% calcium, 14% iron, 16% vit A, 2% vit C, 7% folate.

fancy brunch ideas

Roasted Asparagus With Poached Eggs & Champagne Beurre Blanc

This elegant dish makes a splashy main at a celebratory brunch. Try it in the springtime when tender asparagus stalks are just coming into season.

1½ lb (675 g) **asparagus**

1 tbsp **extra-virgin olive oil**

¼ tsp each **salt** and **pepper**

1 tsp **vinegar**

8 **eggs**

4 **English muffins**

8 oz (225 g) **shaved prosciutto**

CHAMPAGNE BEURRE BLANC:

1 **shallot,** minced

1 cup **Champagne,** dry sparkling white wine or dry white wine (see Tip, opposite)

3 tbsp **Champagne vinegar** or white wine vinegar

¼ tsp **pepper**

¾ cup cold **butter,** cubed

1 tbsp minced **fresh tarragon** or fresh chives

CHAMPAGNE BEURRE BLANC: In small saucepan, boil shallot, Champagne, vinegar and pepper until reduced to 2 tbsp, about 10 minutes. Reduce heat to low. Being careful not to boil, whisk in 1 cube of butter at a time just until melted. *(Make-ahead: Cover and set aside for up to 1 hour. Use at room temperature or rewarm in bowl over saucepan of hot water, whisking often.)* Stir in tarragon.

Snap off woody ends of asparagus; place stalks on rimmed baking sheet. Sprinkle with oil, salt and pepper; shake pan to coat. Roast in 425°F (220°C) oven, shaking pan halfway through, until tender-crisp, about 15 minutes.

Meanwhile, pour enough boiling water into skillet to come 3 inches (8 cm) up side; return to boil. Add vinegar; reduce heat to gentle simmer. Break each egg into small dish; gently slip into simmering water. Cook until desired doneness, about 5 minutes for soft yolks and firm whites. Remove with slotted spoon and drain well, patting bottom of spoon with towel to dry egg.

Meanwhile, halve and toast English muffins. Place 2 halves on each plate; top each with prosciutto, then roasted asparagus, poached egg and about 2 tbsp beurre blanc.

Makes 4 servings. PER SERVING: about 765 cal, 31 g pro, 54 g total fat (27 g sat. fat), 35 g carb, 4 g fibre, 494 mg chol, 1,533 mg sodium. % RDI: 19% calcium, 33% iron, 56% vit A, 15% vit C, 126% folate.

Smoked Salmon Salad

Capers and smoked salmon are great on bagels, but they're even better as accents in this fresh, leafy salad.

3 oz (85 g) thinly sliced **smoked salmon**

8 cups torn **leaf lettuce**

2 **green onions,** sliced

2 tbsp drained **capers**

DRESSING:

2 tbsp **vegetable oil**

1 tsp grated **lemon zest**

1 tbsp **lemon juice**

1 tbsp **liquid honey**

1 tbsp **Dijon mustard**

1 tbsp **white wine vinegar**

¼ tsp each **salt** and **pepper**

DRESSING: In bowl, whisk together oil, lemon zest, lemon juice, honey, mustard, vinegar, salt and pepper. Mince half of the smoked salmon; add to dressing.

In salad bowl, toss together lettuce, green onions and dressing until coated. Divide among plates.

Cut remaining salmon into strips; curl into rosettes and arrange on salad. Sprinkle capers over top.

Makes 4 servings. PER SERVING: about 130 cal, 6 g pro, 8 g total fat (1 g sat. fat), 10 g carb, 2 g fibre, 5 mg chol, 444 mg sodium. % RDI: 8% calcium, 14% iron, 22% vit A, 40% vit C, 28% folate.

Pineapple Mimosa For a

nonalcoholic version of this sunny drink, replace the wine with sparkling white grape juice or ginger ale.

2 oz (¼ cup) **pineapple juice**

3 oz (6 tbsp) **sparkling dry white wine** or Champagne (see Tip, below)

Fresh pineapple spear

Pour pineapple juice into champagne flute; top with wine. Garnish rim with pineapple spear.

Makes 1 serving. PER SERVING: about 91 cal, trace pro, 0 g total fat (0 g sat. fat), 9 g carb, trace fibre, 0 mg chol, 5 mg sodium. % RDI: 2% calcium, 3% iron, 23% vit C, 6% folate.

best **TIPS** ever

Champagne is ideal for making the beurre blanc (opposite) and mimosa (above), but it's pricey. For similar quality at an easier-to-bear cost, try a Canadian sparkling white wine, Italian Prosecco or Spanish cava. In any case, make sure it's labelled *brut,* or dry – less-sweet wine is better for both recipes.

Breakfast in a Cookie

This recipe originally appeared in the *Kid Approved Cookbook,* a project launched by the Kids Eat Smart Foundation of Newfoundland and Labrador. It's an easy-to-eat breakfast for busy mornings.

2 **eggs**

½ cup **liquid honey**

¼ cup **butter,** melted

1 cup grated **carrots**

1 cup coarsely chopped **walnuts**

½ cup **raisins**

½ cup finely chopped **dried apricots**

½ cup chopped **dates**

1 cup **all-purpose flour**

1 cup **quick-cooking rolled oats** (not instant)

¾ tsp **cinnamon**

¾ tsp **nutmeg**

½ tsp **baking soda**

¼ tsp **salt**

1½ cups **oat cereal rounds,**
    such as Cheerios

In large bowl, whisk together eggs, honey and butter until smooth. Stir in carrots, walnuts, raisins, apricots and dates.

In separate large bowl, whisk together flour, oats, cinnamon, nutmeg, baking soda and salt; stir in cereal. Add to egg mixture; stir until moistened and no streaks of dry ingredients remain.

Drop by rounded 1 tbsp, about 1 inch (2.5 cm) apart, onto 2 parchment paper–lined rimless baking sheets. Bake in top and bottom thirds of 350°F (180°C) oven, switching and rotating pans halfway through, until firm to the touch, about 15 minutes.

Let cool on pans on racks for 2 minutes. Transfer to racks; let cool. *(Make-ahead: Store in airtight container for up to 2 days or layer between waxed paper in airtight container and freeze for up to 2 weeks.)*

Makes 30 cookies. PER COOKIE: about 72 cal, 2 g pro, 3 g total fat (1 g sat. fat), 11 g carb, 1 g fibre, 10 mg chol, 43 mg sodium, 73 mg potassium. % RDI: 1% calcium, 4% iron, 5% vit A, 5% folate.

quick breakfast ideas

Baked Egg Cups

Self-contained ramekins full of tasty eggs, peppers, ham and cheese are perfect for breakfast in bed. If you're the cook, they're quick to make, so you can relax with your morning coffee while they bake.

4 slices **Black Forest ham,**
   smoked turkey or beef salami
½ cup chopped **sweet green pepper**
4 **eggs**
¼ tsp **pepper**
⅓ cup shredded **Cheddar cheese** or
   mozzarella cheese

Trim each ham slice to make 5-inch (12 cm) circle. Dice ham scraps; set aside.

Fit 1 slice of the ham into each of 4 greased 3-inch (125 mL) ramekins or custard cups. Divide green pepper among ramekins; crack 1 of the eggs into each. Sprinkle with reserved ham, pepper and Cheddar cheese.

Place ramekins on baking sheet. Bake in 375°F (190°C) oven until whites are set, yolks are still runny and cheese is bubbly, about 15 minutes. Let cool for 5 minutes before serving.

Makes 4 servings. PER SERVING: about 147 cal, 13 g pro, 9 g total fat (4 g sat. fat), 3 g carb, trace fibre, 206 mg chol, 435 mg sodium, 197 mg potassium. % RDI: 9% calcium, 8% iron, 13% vit A, 22% vit C, 15% folate.

Grainy Porridge

The dry mix makes 4 cups, so you'll have almost a week's worth of breakfasts ready to go.

Pinch **salt**

GRAINY PORRIDGE MIX:

1 cup **barley flakes** (see Tips, below)

1 cup **rye flakes**

1 cup **large-flake rolled oats** (not instant)

1 cup **steel-cut oats**

GRAINY PORRIDGE MIX: Combine barley flakes, rye flakes, large-flake oats and steel-cut oats. *(Make-ahead: Store in airtight container for up to 1 month.)*

In saucepan, bring 3 cups water and salt to boil; stir in 1 cup of the porridge mix (save remainder for other breakfasts). Reduce heat, cover and simmer until thickened, 10 minutes.

Makes 4 servings. PER SERVING: about 101 cal, 4 g pro, 1 g total fat (trace sat. fat), 21 g carb, 3 g fibre, 0 mg chol, 5 mg sodium. % RDI: 1% calcium, 7% iron, 3% folate.

Chewy Apple Berry Smoothie

Apple skins, wheat bran and berries all give this smoothie a hefty, healthy dose of fibre.

2 **Golden Delicious apples** (unpeeled), diced

1 cup **milk**

½ cup each **frozen blueberries** and **frozen strawberries**

½ cup **plain yogurt**

2 tbsp **wheat bran**

2 tsp **liquid honey**

In blender, purée apples with milk for 2 minutes.

Add blueberries, strawberries, yogurt, wheat bran and honey; purée until smooth.

Makes 2 servings. PER SERVING: about 247 cal, 8 g pro, 5 g total fat (3 g sat. fat), 47 g carb, 6 g fibre, 15 mg chol, 100 mg sodium. % RDI: 24% calcium, 8% iron, 9% vit A, 43% vit C, 13% folate.

best **TIPS** ever

- Look for whole grain rolled flakes – including barley, rye and oats – and steel-cut oats at your local bulk food store or in packages in the health food aisle of the supermarket. Keep your whole grain pantry staples fresh by sealing them in airtight containers and storing them in the freezer. Canning jars and resealable freezer bags both work well.

- Serve this porridge with your favourite toppings: milk, maple syrup, honey and/or butter. For a treat, add a handful of dried fruit to the water with the porridge mix.

on the go

Tropical Granola Clusters With Brazil Nuts

Although known as nuts, Brazil nuts are actually seeds. But whatever you call them, they're a rich, nutritious addition to tempting little granola bites.

2 cups **large-flake rolled oats**

1 cup sliced **Brazil nuts**

½ cup **unsalted hulled sunflower seeds**

1 cup chopped **mixed dried tropical fruit**
   (such as pineapple, mango and papaya)

½ cup **sweetened shredded coconut**

½ cup **liquid honey**

¼ cup packed **brown sugar**

2 tbsp **vegetable oil**

1 tsp **vanilla**

¼ tsp **salt**

Combine oats, Brazil nuts and sunflower seeds; spread on rimmed baking sheet. Bake in 350°F (180°C) oven, stirring once, until light golden, about 15 minutes. Transfer to bowl. Stir in tropical fruit and coconut.

In saucepan over medium heat, melt together honey, brown sugar, oil, vanilla and salt; stir into oat mixture. Press into parchment paper–lined 8-inch (2 L) square cake pan.

Bake in 300°F (150°C) oven until golden and firm to the touch, about 30 minutes. Let cool for 20 minutes. Break into bite-size clusters; let cool completely. *(Make-ahead: Store in airtight container for up to 5 days.)*

Makes about 40 pieces. PER PIECE: about 84 cal, 2 g pro, 4 g total fat (1 g sat. fat), 12 g carb, 1 g fibre, 0 mg chol, 19 mg sodium, 92 mg potassium. % RDI: 1% calcium, 4% iron, 1% vit A, 5% vit C, 2% folate.

Lightened-Up Hummus

Pack this nutritious dip with vegetable sticks and whole grain pita wedges for a quick and wholesome lunch. Or have it as a late afternoon pick-me-up that will tide you over till dinner.

¾ cup **fat-free plain yogurt**

1 can (19 oz/540 mL) **chickpeas,** drained and rinsed

2 tbsp **lemon juice**

1 tbsp **sesame oil**

1 tsp **ground cumin**

¼ tsp **salt**

Pinch **cayenne pepper**

2 cloves **garlic,** minced

1 tbsp **extra-virgin olive oil**

Pinch **sweet paprika**

Line small sieve with cheesecloth; set over bowl. Add yogurt; drain in refrigerator until reduced by half, about 2 hours.

In food processor, purée together yogurt, chickpeas, lemon juice, sesame oil, cumin, salt and cayenne pepper until smooth; scrape into bowl. Stir in garlic. *(Make-ahead: Cover and refrigerate for up to 3 days.)*

Drizzle olive oil over hummus; sprinkle with paprika.

Makes 2 cups. PER 1 TBSP: about 26 cal, 1 g pro, 1 g total fat (trace sat. fat), 3 g carb, 1 g fibre, 0 mg chol, 55 mg sodium. % RDI: 1% calcium, 1% iron, 2% vit C, 4% folate.

best TIPS ever

Authentic hummus recipes include lots of tahini (sesame seed paste) and olive oil. While those are healthy ingredients, they are still high in fat and calories. Here, tahini is replaced with a much smaller amount of sesame oil and a drizzle of olive oil. A typical 2 tbsp serving of hummus has about 89 calories and 5.8 grams of fat, but this one, lightened up with calcium-rich yogurt, has only 52 calories and 2 grams of fat.

Pineapple Berry Smoothies
A jar of homemade smoothie is the ultimate portable snack. Try one for a midmorning energy boost.

2 cups **frozen mixed berries**

Half **banana**

1 cup **pineapple juice**

1 to 2 tsp **liquid honey** (optional)

In blender, purée together berries, banana and pineapple juice until smooth. Sweeten with honey, if using.

Makes 2 servings. PER SERVING: about 190 cal, 2 g pro, 1 g total fat (0 g sat. fat), 47 g carb, 9 g fibre, 0 mg chol, 2 mg sodium. % RDI: 5% calcium, 11% iron, 88% vit C, 16% folate.

Carrot Salad Bites
These healthy tidbits make a wonderful snack. Topped with edible violets, they're a beautiful appetizer.

1½ cups grated **carrots**

1 tbsp **lemon juice**

1 tbsp **olive oil**

Pinch each **salt** and **pepper**

⅓ cup **herbed cream cheese**

12 slices **cocktail rye bread**

Fresh parsley sprigs

Violets (optional)

Stir together carrots, lemon juice, oil, salt and pepper. *(Make-ahead: Cover and refrigerate for up to 24 hours.)*

Spread cream cheese over each bread slice; divide carrot mixture among slices. Garnish with sprig of parsley, and violets (if using).

Makes 12 servings. PER SERVING: about 57 cal, 1 g pro, 3 g total fat (1 g sat. fat), 7 g carb, 1 g fibre, 5 mg chol, 98 mg sodium, 75 mg potassium. % RDI: 2% calcium, 3% iron, 25% vit A, 3% vit C, 1% folate.

Honey Apple Snack Mix

A little sweet and a little salty, this party mix is a hit with kids (and grown-ups, who might enjoy it with cocktails). Make it with walnuts and almonds instead of the peanuts and pecans if you prefer.

4 cups **woven wheat cereal squares**
(such as Shreddies)

3 **rice cakes,** broken in small pieces

1 cup **pretzel sticks**

½ cup each **unsalted roasted peanuts**
and **pecan pieces**

2 tbsp packed **brown sugar**

2½ tsp **garlic powder**

1¼ tsp **chili powder**

Pinch **salt**

⅓ cup **unsweetened applesauce**

3 tbsp **butter**

2 tbsp **liquid honey**

In bowl, combine cereal squares, rice cakes, pretzels, peanuts, pecans, brown sugar, garlic powder, chili powder and salt.

In small saucepan, heat applesauce, butter and honey over medium-low heat until butter is melted, about 2 minutes. Stir into cereal mixture, tossing to coat. Spread on rimmed baking sheet.

Bake in 325°F (160°C) oven, stirring occasionally, until cereal squares are deep golden, 18 to 20 minutes. Let cool. *(Make-ahead: Store in airtight container for up to 5 days.)*

Makes 8 cups. PER ¼ CUP: about 76 cal, 2 g pro, 4 g total fat (1 g sat. fat), 10 g carb, 1 g fibre, 3 mg chol, 77 mg sodium, 58 mg potassium. % RDI: 1% calcium, 8% iron, 1% vit A, 4% folate.

Toasted Tootsies in Blankets
Serve these warm pigs in blankets with barbecue sauce, smooth salsa or ketchup for dipping.

12 slices **white bread**

¼ cup **sweet mustard**

¾ cup minced **onion**

12 **all-beef hotdogs** (1 lb/450 g)

2 tbsp **butter,** melted, or vegetable oil

Cut crusts off bread. Using rolling pin, roll each slice to ⅛-inch (3 mm) thickness. Brush with mustard; sprinkle with onion. Place 1 hotdog on edge of each slice; roll up tightly to enclose. *(Make-ahead: Layer between waxed paper in airtight container and refrigerate for up to 2 days or freeze for up to 3 weeks.)*

Place, seam side down, on parchment paper–lined or greased rimmed baking sheet; brush with butter. Bake in 400°F (200°C) oven, turning once, until bread is crisp, 20 to 25 minutes. Cut each in half.

Makes 24 pieces. PER PIECE: 100 cal, 3 g pro, 6 g total fat (2 g sat. fat), 8 g carb, trace fibre, 15 mg chol, 240 mg sodium. % RDI: 1% calcium, 4% iron, 1% vit A, 4% folate.

change it up
Mustard & Relish Toasted Tootsies in Blankets: Replace onion with dill pickle relish.

Creamy Cantaloupe Pops
Ice pops are a definite kid magnet. These are the perfect combo of fruit and cream, with just a hint of tanginess.

2 cups chopped **cantaloupe** (about one-quarter cantaloupe)

½ cup **orange juice**

½ cup **Balkan-style plain yogurt**

½ cup **sour cream**

2 tbsp **liquid honey**

In food processor or blender, purée cantaloupe until smooth. Add orange juice, yogurt, sour cream and honey; purée until combined.

Pour into ice-pop moulds; freeze until firm, about 3 hours. *(Make-ahead: Freeze for up to 3 days.)*

Makes 8 to 10 servings. PER EACH OF 10 SERVINGS: about 57 cal, 1 g pro, 2 g total fat (2 g sat. fat), 9 g carb, trace fibre, 7 mg chol, 16 mg sodium, 145 mg potassium. % RDI: 3% calcium, 1% iron, 13% vit A, 28% vit C, 6% folate.

change it up
Ginger Melon Ice Pops: Add 1 tsp grated fresh ginger to chopped melon; purée.

best
TIPS
ever

• For the most flavourful melon, choose one that feels heavy for its size and has a sweet scent.

• Mixing the sour cream with Balkan-style yogurt ensures a creamy texture. Other types of yogurt, such as Greek yogurt, can be chalky.

• No ice-pop moulds? Use small paper cups and wooden sticks. Just peel off the cups when the kids are ready to eat.

S'mores Popcorn Balls Two of the best snacks ever – s'mores and popcorn – become one single delicious package. These balls are almost as much fun to make as they are to eat, so get the kids in the kitchen to help.

10 cups popped **popcorn**
(about ½ cup unpopped)
2 cups pieces (½ inch/1 cm) **graham crackers** (about 15 crackers)
1 bag (250 g) **mini marshmallows**
(about 6 cups)
¼ cup **butter**
1 tsp **vanilla**

TOPPING:

2 oz (60 g) **bittersweet chocolate,**
finely chopped

In large greased roasting pan, toss together popcorn, graham crackers and 1 cup of the marshmallows. Set aside.

In large saucepan, melt remaining marshmallows with butter over medium-low heat, stirring constantly, until smooth. Remove from heat. Stir in vanilla. Immediately pour over popcorn mixture; stir with greased spatula to coat.

Let cool enough to handle. With greased hands, form by ¾ cupfuls into balls. Place on waxed paper–lined baking sheet; let cool.

TOPPING: In heatproof bowl over saucepan of hot (not boiling) water, melt chocolate. Using fork, drizzle half of the chocolate all over popcorn balls; refrigerate until set, about 10 minutes.

Turn balls over and drizzle with remaining chocolate; refrigerate until set, about 10 minutes. *(Make-ahead: Wrap individually in plastic wrap and store for up to 24 hours.)*

Makes 12 pieces. PER PIECE: about 190 cal, 2 g pro, 7 g total fat (4 g sat. fat), 31 g carb, 2 g fibre, 10 mg chol, 91 mg sodium, 61 mg potassium. % RDI: 1% calcium, 6% iron, 4% vit A, 3% folate.

Cobb-Style Chicken Sandwich

Sometimes your lunch box needs a gourmet touch. Inspired by the rich salad of the same name, this sandwich steps up your lunch game. Pack all the components and cut the avocado right before you assemble the sandwich to keep it from turning brown.

6 slices **bacon,** halved

2 **boneless skinless chicken breasts**

¼ tsp each **salt** and **pepper**

4 **soft buns,** halved

4 leaves **red leaf lettuce**

1 **tomato,** sliced

1 **avocado,** peeled and thinly sliced

BLUE CHEESE MAYONNAISE:

3 tbsp **light mayonnaise**

1 oz (30 g) **blue cheese,** crumbled

1 tsp **red wine vinegar**

½ tsp **Dijon mustard**

Pinch **pepper**

BLUE CHEESE MAYONNAISE: Stir together mayonnaise, blue cheese, vinegar, mustard and pepper; set aside.

In large skillet, cook bacon over medium heat until crisp, about 6 minutes. Transfer to paper towel–lined plate; set aside. Drain all but 1 tbsp fat from pan.

With knife held horizontally, cut chicken breasts in half to make 4 flat pieces. Sprinkle with salt and pepper. In same skillet, cook chicken, turning once, until no longer pink inside, about 8 minutes.

Spread cut sides of buns with blue cheese mayonnaise. Top bottom halves with lettuce, tomato, avocado, chicken and bacon. Sandwich with tops of buns.

Makes 4 servings. PER SERVING: about 437 cal, 26 g pro, 25 g total fat (7 g sat. fat), 30 g carb, 5 g fibre, 62 mg chol, 827 mg sodium, 660 mg potassium. % RDI: 10% calcium, 17% iron, 13% vit A, 15% vit C, 45% folate.

hearty packed lunches

Wild Rice Mushroom Soup

This velvety, nutty-textured soup tastes almost too rich to be meatless, but it is! For a slightly thinner, dairy-free version, replace butter with olive oil and replace cream with almond, rice or soy milk.

½ cup **wild rice**

1¼ tsp **salt**

1 pkg (½ oz/14 g) **dried porcini mushrooms**

1 cup **boiling water**

2 tbsp **butter**

1 tbsp **vegetable oil**

4 cups sliced **cremini mushrooms**

¼ cup **brandy** or vegetable broth

2 cups diced **onions**

2 cups diced **celery**

2 cloves **garlic,** minced

1 tbsp chopped **fresh thyme**

¼ tsp **pepper**

2 cups **vegetable broth**

¼ cup **whipping cream (35%)**

In saucepan, bring 2 cups water, wild rice and ½ tsp of the salt to boil over high heat. Reduce heat and simmer, covered, until most of the rice is split and tender, about 45 minutes. Remove from heat; let stand for 5 minutes. Drain. *(Make-ahead: Refrigerate in airtight container for up to 2 days.)*

Soak porcinis in boiling water until softened, about 30 minutes. Reserving soaking liquid, strain; discard sediment. Chop porcinis.

In skillet, heat half of the butter with the oil over medium-high heat; sauté porcini and cremini mushrooms and ¼ tsp of the remaining salt until golden, about 5 minutes.

Add brandy; cook until most of the liquid is evaporated, about 1 minute.

In large saucepan, melt remaining butter over medium heat; fry onions, celery, garlic, thyme, pepper and remaining salt, stirring often, until very soft, about 10 minutes.

Add reserved soaking liquid, broth and 2 cups water; bring to boil. Reduce heat and simmer, stirring occasionally, for 20 minutes. Stir in mushroom mixture; let cool slightly.

In blender, purée half of the soup; return to pan. Stir in wild rice and cream; bring to simmer over medium heat, stirring often. *(Make-ahead: Refrigerate in airtight container for up to 2 days.)*

Makes 6 servings. PER SERVING: about 198 cal, 5 g pro, 10 g total fat (5 g sat. fat), 22 g carb, 4 g fibre, 26 mg chol, 1,018 mg sodium. % RDI: 5% calcium, 6% iron, 8% vit A, 12% vit C, 18% folate.

Tuna & Bean Salad

Filling and satisfying, this salad is a great alternative to the usual tuna sandwich in your brown bag. If you have black beans, try substituting them for the red kidney beans for a Southwestern twist.

3 tbsp **lemon juice**

1 tbsp **vegetable oil**

1 tsp **sesame oil**

1 clove **garlic,** minced

¼ tsp **ground cumin**

¼ tsp each **salt** and **pepper**

1 can (19 oz/540 mL) **red kidney beans,** drained and rinsed

1 can (6 oz/170 g) **tuna,** drained and broken in large chunks

Half **sweet red pepper,** diced

⅔ cup diced **English cucumber**

⅔ cup **frozen corn kernels,** cooked and cooled

3 tbsp minced **fresh mint**

In bowl, whisk together lemon juice, vegetable oil, sesame oil, garlic, cumin, salt and pepper. Toss in kidney beans, tuna, red pepper, cucumber, corn and mint.

Makes 4 servings. PER SERVING: about 242 cal, 17 g pro, 8 g total fat (1 g sat. fat), 26 g carb, 9 g fibre, 6 mg chol, 612 mg sodium, 485 mg potassium. % RDI: 4% calcium, 19% iron, 8% vit A, 42% vit C, 34% folate.

best **TIPS** ever

• Lunch prep is a lot easier when you have the right equipment. Watch for sales and stock up on airtight containers in assorted sizes. Glass dishes with silicone lids are versatile – they can go into the fridge, freezer, microwave and dishwasher without worry. Good old-fashioned canning jars are great for toting soups and other liquids – you can even buy special lids with sipper spouts for drinks.

• Keep cold lunch items cold with ice packs or frozen juice boxes. For hot lunch items, invest in a good vacuum flask (Thermos) to ensure dishes stay piping hot.

Banana Chocolate Chip Muffins

These moist, yummy muffins pair two of the most popular flavours. They make a tasty treat tucked into your kids' lunch boxes.

2½ cups **all-purpose flour**

1 cup packed **brown sugar**

1½ tsp **baking powder**

1 tsp **baking soda**

½ tsp **salt**

2 **eggs**

1 cup **buttermilk**

1 cup mashed **bananas**

⅓ cup **vegetable oil**

1 tsp **vanilla**

¾ cup **chocolate chips**

In large bowl, whisk together flour, brown sugar, baking powder, baking soda and salt. In separate bowl, beat eggs; blend in buttermilk, bananas, oil and vanilla. Pour over dry ingredients; sprinkle with chocolate chips. Stir just until dry ingredients are moistened.

Spoon into greased or paper-lined muffin cups, filling three-quarters full. Bake in 375°F (190°C) oven until tops are firm to the touch, 20 to 25 minutes. Let cool in pan on rack for 5 minutes; transfer to rack and let cool.

Makes 12 muffins. PER MUFFIN: about 305 cal, 5 g pro, 11 g total fat (3 g sat. fat), 50 g carb, 2 g fibre, 32 mg chol, 264 mg sodium. % RDI: 6% calcium, 14% iron, 2% vit A, 2% vit C, 16% folate.

Extraterrestrial Tuna Sandwiches

These small pitas stuffed with tuna filling look like fun flying saucers – perfect for lunch boxes and kids' parties. You'll need two packages (6 oz/175 g each) of mini pitas.

2 cans (6 oz/170 g each) **tuna,**
 drained
1 rib **celery,** diced
1 **carrot,** diced
⅓ cup **light mayonnaise**
3 tbsp **unsalted roasted hulled**
 pumpkin seeds
12 **seedless green grapes,** quartered
¼ tsp each **salt** and **pepper**
24 **mini whole wheat pitas** (2½ inches/6 cm)

Stir together tuna, celery, carrot, mayonnaise, pumpkin seeds, grapes, salt and pepper. *(Make-ahead: Cover and refrigerate for up to 24 hours.)*

Cut 2-inch (5 cm) circle from 1 side of each mini pita to make container. Spoon rounded 1 tbsp tuna mixture into each hole.

Makes 24 sandwiches. PER SANDWICH: about 62 cal, 4 g pro, 2 g total fat (trace sat. fat), 7 g carb, 1 g fibre, 5 mg chol, 138 mg sodium. % RDI: 1% calcium, 6% iron, 5% vit A, 2% vit C, 3% folate.

Fruit Kabobs With Creamy Berry Dip
Some kids (and adults) need coaxing to enjoy fruit. This creamy, tangy dip does the trick.

¼ cup **light cream cheese**

½ cup **light sour cream**

2 tbsp **seedless raspberry jam** or
  strawberry jam

1 **red-skinned apple**

1 **pear**

1 cup **seedless green grapes**

Place cream cheese in microwaveable bowl; microwave on high until softened, about 20 seconds. Whisk in sour cream and jam until smooth.

Cut apple and pear into bite-size chunks; thread chunks and grapes onto 4 skewers. Serve with dip.

Makes 4 servings. PER SERVING: about 166 cal, 4 g pro, 5 g total fat (3 g sat. fat), 29 g carb, 2 g fibre, 14 mg chol, 131 mg sodium. % RDI: 8% calcium, 2% iron, 4% vit A, 15% vit C, 4% folate.

change it up

Strawberry Banana Split Kabobs With Creamy Chocolate Dip: Replace apple, pear and grapes with 2 bananas, cut in chunks, and 1½ cups hulled strawberries. Replace jam with ¼ cup chocolate sauce.

Melon Kabobs With Creamy Berry Dip: Replace apple, pear and grapes with 1 cup each cubed peeled cantaloupe, honeydew melon and watermelon.

Tropical Fruit Kabobs With Creamy Orange Dip: Replace apple, pear and grapes with 1 mango and 2 kiwifruit, peeled and cut into chunks, and 1 cup pineapple chunks. Replace jam with orange juice concentrate.

Peach Leather
Chewy and intensely peachy, this leather is made with just fruit and sugar, so it's healthier than store-bought.

4 cups chopped (unpeeled) **peaches** or
  nectarines (about 5)

2 tbsp **granulated sugar**

In blender or food processor, purée peaches with sugar until smooth to make about 3 cups.

Pour purée into deep saucepan and bring to boil; reduce heat and simmer, stirring often, until reduced by half, about 30 minutes. Let cool to room temperature.

Line 2 rimmed baking sheets with foil; grease foil. Spread ¼ cupfuls of the purée on foil to make six 6-inch (15 cm) circles. Bake in 175°F (80°C) oven, rotating pan halfway through, until no longer sticky in centre, 2 to 3 hours.

Transfer fruit leather on foil to rack; let stand, uncovered, at room temperature overnight or until completely dry. Roll up in plastic wrap. *(Make-ahead: Refrigerate for up to 2 weeks.)*

Makes 6 servings. PER SERVING: about 60 cal, 1 g pro, trace total fat (0 g sat. fat), 15 g carb, 2 g fibre, 0 mg chol, 0 mg sodium, 215 mg potassium. % RDI: 1% calcium, 2% iron, 3% vit A, 8% vit C, 1% folate.

best **TIPS** ever

- Brush the cut sides of fruit with a bit of lemon juice to prevent browning in your kids' lunch boxes.
- Make the cream cheese dip for the fruit kabobs and refrigerate it. Then use an ice pack to keep it cool till lunchtime.

Smoked Ham, Brie & Cranberry Sandwiches

The cranberry sauce or onion marmalade in this sandwich definitely makes it one for adults. For a more kid-friendly lunch, use a fruit spread instead.

2 tbsp **whole-berry cranberry sauce** or onion marmalade

2 **whole wheat kaiser rolls,** halved

4 oz (115 g) thinly sliced **smoked ham**

2 oz (55 g) **Brie cheese,** sliced

2 leaves **lettuce**

Spread cranberry sauce over cut sides of bottom halves of rolls. Divide ham and Brie cheese evenly over cranberry sauce; top with lettuce. Sandwich with tops of rolls.

Makes 2 servings. PER SERVING: about 351 cal, 21 g pro, 12 g total fat (6 g sat. fat), 41 g carb, 5 g fibre, 56 mg chol, 1,112 mg sodium, 435 mg potassium. % RDI: 12% calcium, 16% iron, 12% vit A, 3% vit C, 20% folate.

Roasted Curry Cauliflower Dip

Roasting the cauliflower gives it a deep, rich flavour in this gorgeous dip. Serve with pappadams, crudités or crackers for a change of pace in your brown bag.

¾ cup **Balkan-style plain yogurt**

¼ cup **extra-virgin olive oil**

1 tsp **curry powder**

½ tsp each **salt, ground cumin**
  and **ground coriander**

¼ tsp each **ground ginger**
  and **pepper**

1 head **cauliflower** (2½ lb/1.125 kg)

1 large **onion,** cut in eighths

6 cloves **garlic**

1 tbsp **lemon juice**

3 tbsp chopped **fresh cilantro**
  or fresh chives

In large bowl, stir together ⅓ cup of the yogurt, oil, curry powder, salt, cumin, coriander, ginger and pepper. Cut cauliflower into florets; add to yogurt mixture along with onion and garlic, tossing to coat.

Spread on large foil-lined rimmed baking sheet; roast in 425°F (220°C) oven, stirring once, until tender and browned, about 40 minutes. Let cool.

In food processor, purée together cauliflower mixture, remaining yogurt and lemon juice until fairly smooth with a few chunks remaining. Stir in cilantro. *(Make-ahead: Refrigerate in airtight container for up to 2 days.)*

Makes 3 cups. PER 2 TBSP: about 38 cal, 1 g pro, 3 g total fat (1 g sat. fat), 3 g carb, 1 g fibre, 1 mg chol, 56 mg sodium, 65 mg potassium. % RDI: 2% calcium, 1% iron, 1% vit A, 18% vit C, 5% folate.

Mediterranean Fusilli Salad

This gourmet bean and pasta salad – packed with summery flavours – brightens up your lunch hour.

12 oz (340 g) **fusilli pasta**

1 **zucchini,** cubed

1 can (19 oz/540 mL) **romano beans,**
   drained and rinsed

⅔ cup sliced drained **oil-packed sun-dried tomatoes**

¾ cup thinly sliced **fresh basil**

DRESSING:

⅔ cup **extra-virgin olive oil**

¼ cup **red wine vinegar**

1 clove **garlic,** minced

1 tsp each **ground cumin** and
   dried oregano

¼ tsp each **salt** and **pepper**

DRESSING: Whisk together oil, vinegar, garlic, cumin, oregano, salt and pepper. Set aside.

In large pot of boiling salted water, cook fusilli according to package instructions until al dente. Drain and rinse under cold water; drain well and place in large bowl. Add zucchini, beans and tomatoes; pour dressing over top and toss to combine. *(Make-ahead: Cover and refrigerate for up to 24 hours.)*

Toss with basil just before serving.

Makes 12 servings. PER SERVING: about 263 cal, 6 g pro, 14 g total fat (2 g sat. fat), 30 g carb, 4 g fibre, 0 mg chol, 252 mg sodium. % RDI: 3% calcium, 16% iron, 3% vit A, 15% vit C, 41% folate.

Kale & Chickpea Soup

Freeze portions of this satisfying soup for weekday lunches. Add a slice of crusty bread to sop up every drop of broth.

2 tbsp **extra-virgin olive oil**

1 **onion,** chopped

2 cloves **garlic,** minced

¼ tsp crumbled **dried sage**

½ tsp each **salt** and **pepper**

3 cups **sodium-reduced chicken broth**

2 cups cubed peeled **sweet potato**

1½ cups cubed **Black Forest ham**
   (about 6 oz/170 g)

1 **sweet red pepper,** chopped

1 can (19 oz/540 mL) **chickpeas,**
   drained and rinsed

3 cups chopped stemmed **kale**
   (see Tip, below)

In large saucepan, heat oil over medium heat; fry onion, garlic, sage, salt and pepper, stirring occasionally, until onion is softened, about 5 minutes.

Add broth, 3 cups water, sweet potato, ham, red pepper and chickpeas; bring to boil. Reduce heat, cover and simmer until potato is tender, about 15 minutes.

Add kale; simmer until tender, about 5 minutes. *(Make-ahead: Refrigerate in airtight containers for up to 3 days or freeze for up to 1 month.)*

Makes 6 servings. PER SERVING: about 260 cal, 14 g pro, 8 g total fat (1 g sat. fat), 34 g carb, 5 g fibre, 14 mg chol, 830 mg sodium. % RDI: 8% calcium, 17% iron, 110% vit A, 130% vit C, 30% folate.

change it up

Spinach & Chickpea Soup: Substitute spinach for kale; cook until wilted, about 1 minute.

best **TIPS** ever

Kale is a vitamin- and fibre-packed superfood. This recipe uses only about half a bunch. Shred the remainder and add to salads. Or tear leaves, toss with a little oil and your favourite seasonings, and bake in 350°F (180°C) oven until crispy and dark green, 12 to 15 minutes.

Smoked Salmon & Radish Dip
Dip is fantastic for a potluck. It's portable and everyone loves it on crackers, croûtes and veggies. This one tastes luxuriously creamy, but it's lightened up with low-fat pressed cottage cheese.

¾ cup **sour cream** or light sour cream

½ cup **low-fat pressed cottage cheese**

½ cup **cream cheese** or
   light cream cheese, softened

Pinch each **salt** and **pepper**

4 oz (115 g) **smoked salmon,**
   finely chopped

½ cup finely chopped **red radishes**
   (about half bunch)

⅓ cup finely chopped **red onion**

2 tbsp chopped **fresh chives** (optional)

In large bowl, beat together sour cream, cottage cheese, cream cheese, salt and pepper. Stir in salmon, radishes, onion, and chives (if using). Transfer to serving bowl. *(Make-ahead: Cover and refrigerate for up to 2 days. Let stand at room temperature for 30 minutes before serving.)*

Makes about 2 cups. PER 1 TBSP: about 30 cal, 2 g pro, 2 g total fat (1 g sat. fat), 1 g carb, trace fibre, 7 mg chol, 42 mg sodium. % RDI: 1% calcium, 1% iron, 2% vit A, 2% vit C, 1% folate.

best potluck recipes

Slow Cooker Chocolate Chili Pulled Pork

Pulled pork gets an exotic makeover with an easy-to-make Mexican mole-style sauce. Tote the whole slow cooker with you to a potluck to keep the pork warm on the buffet.

3 **onions,** chopped

4 cloves **garlic,** minced

1½ cups **bottled strained tomatoes**
   (passata)

⅓ cup **cider vinegar**

¼ cup **chili powder**

¼ cup **fancy molasses**

2 tbsp packed **dark brown sugar**

1 tsp **dried oregano**

1 tsp each **ground cumin** and
   ground coriander

½ tsp **salt**

¼ tsp **pepper**

2 oz (60 g) **unsweetened chocolate,**
   chopped

3 lb (1.35 kg) **boneless pork shoulder roast**

In slow cooker, combine onions, garlic, tomatoes, ½ cup water, vinegar, chili powder, molasses, brown sugar, oregano, cumin, coriander, salt and pepper; stir in chocolate. Add pork, turning to coat.

Cover and cook on low until pork is tender, 6 to 8 hours.

Transfer pork to bowl. With 2 forks, shred or "pull" pork. Skim fat from liquid in slow cooker. Stir pork back into liquid.

Makes 8 servings. PER SERVING: about 484 cal, 31 g pro, 31 g total fat (12 g sat. fat), 23 g carb, 3 g fibre, 112 mg chol, 379 mg sodium, 938 mg potassium. % RDI: 7% calcium, 38% iron, 12% vit A, 8% vit C, 10% folate.

best
TIPS
ever

- For the most authentic taste experience, serve Slow Cooker Chocolate Chili Pulled Pork (above) in warm corn tortillas. A side of refried beans and a simple green salad make this a complete Mexican feast. It's a tasty serve-yourself option at a buffet.

- Whole wheat couscous is higher in fibre than regular couscous but tastes pretty much the same. It's delicious as a side dish, in stuffings and in grain salads, such as our Couscous & Three-Bean Salad (opposite). Try it in place of white couscous in your favourite recipes.

Couscous & Three-Bean Salad

Whole grain couscous, beans and veggies make this portable salad ultra-healthy.

½ cup each cut (½ inch/1 cm) **green beans**
  and diced **carrots**
1 **sweet yellow pepper,** diced
1 cup **whole wheat couscous**
  (see Tips, opposite)
⅔ cup **cooked chickpeas** or rinsed
  drained canned chickpeas
⅔ cup rinsed drained canned
  red kidney beans
1 **green onion,** thinly sliced
¼ cup **extra-virgin olive oil**
½ tsp grated **lemon zest**
3 tbsp **lemon juice**
1 tsp **Dijon mustard**
½ tsp each **dried oregano** and **salt**
¼ tsp **pepper**

In saucepan, bring 2 cups water to boil; boil green beans, carrots and yellow pepper for 2 minutes. Reserving cooking liquid, drain. In large bowl, stir couscous with 1 cup of the reserved cooking liquid; cover and let stand for 5 minutes. Add vegetables, chickpeas, kidney beans and green onion.

Whisk together oil, lemon zest, lemon juice, mustard, oregano, salt and pepper. Pour over couscous mixture and toss to combine. *(Make-ahead: Refrigerate in airtight container for up to 2 days.)*

Makes 4 to 6 servings. PER EACH OF 6 SERVINGS: about 267 cal, 8 g pro, 10 g total fat (1 g sat. fat), 38 g carb, 7 g fibre, 0 mg chol, 211 mg sodium. % RDI: 4% calcium, 16% iron, 17% vit A, 58% vit C, 31% folate.

No-Bake Apricot Nuggets

More like fudge than cookies, these bite-size treats are a sweet, simple ending to a meal.

¾ cup packed **brown sugar**
¾ cup **butter**
1 can (300 mL) **sweetened condensed milk**
2 tbsp **lemon juice**
2¾ cups **vanilla wafer crumbs** (about 90 cookies)
¾ cup chopped **dried apricots**
¾ cup **dried cranberries**
¾ cup **unsweetened shredded coconut**

In saucepan, combine brown sugar, butter and condensed milk over medium-low heat, stirring to prevent scorching, until butter is melted. Remove from heat; stir in lemon juice.

In bowl, combine wafer crumbs, apricots, cranberries and ½ cup of the coconut; add butter mixture, stirring until combined. Press into parchment paper–lined 13- x 9-inch (3.5 L) cake pan. Sprinkle with remaining coconut; press gently. Cover and refrigerate until firm, about 4 hours.

Cut into squares. *(Make-ahead: Layer between waxed paper in airtight container and store at room temperature for up to 5 days or freeze for up to 1 month.)*

Makes 40 squares. PER SQUARE: about 121 cal, 1 g pro, 6 g total fat (3 g sat. fat), 17 g carb, 1 g fibre, 17 mg chol, 70 mg sodium. % RDI: 3% calcium, 3% iron, 6% vit A, 2% vit C, 2% folate.

Quinoa & Chickpea Salad With Tomato Vinaigrette

When your evenings are filled with sports practices, meetings and activities, this packable whole grain salad will keep you moving at full speed.

1 cup **quinoa,** rinsed

2 cups chopped trimmed **green beans**

1 can (19 oz/540 mL) **chickpeas,** drained and rinsed

1 **sweet red pepper,** diced

1 cup crumbled **feta cheese**

TOMATO VINAIGRETTE:

⅓ cup **bottled strained tomatoes** (passata)

3 tbsp **red wine vinegar**

3 tbsp **olive oil**

3 tbsp **liquid honey**

½ tsp each **dried Italian herb seasoning** and **salt**

¼ tsp **pepper**

Pinch **cayenne pepper**

In saucepan, bring quinoa and 2 cups water to boil; reduce heat, cover and simmer for 12 minutes. Fluff with fork; let cool.

Meanwhile, in saucepan of boiling salted water, blanch green beans until tender-crisp, about 3 minutes. Drain and chill in ice water. Drain and transfer to large bowl.

Stir in cooled quinoa, chickpeas, red pepper and feta cheese.

TOMATO VINAIGRETTE: Whisk together tomatoes, vinegar, oil, honey, Italian herb seasoning, salt, pepper and cayenne pepper; pour over quinoa mixture and stir to coat.

Makes 4 servings. PER SERVING: about 556 cal, 18 g pro, 22 g total fat (8 g sat. fat), 75 g carb, 9 g fibre, 35 mg chol, 1,155 mg sodium, 649 mg potassium. % RDI: 25% calcium, 46% iron, 18% vit A, 108% vit C, 53% folate.

grab & go dinners

Chicken Club Wrap With Garlic Mayo Simple to tote and even easier to enjoy, this wrap has all the elements of a club sandwich in one handy package. Roll in waxed paper and peel it down as you eat to catch any drips.

8 slices **bacon**

4 **boneless skinless chicken breasts**

½ tsp each **salt** and **pepper**

1 **plum tomato**

4 large **tortillas**

4 leaves **romaine lettuce,** chopped

GARLIC MAYO:

1 large clove **garlic**

Pinch **salt**

¼ cup **light mayonnaise**

1 tsp **lemon juice**

Dash **hot pepper sauce**

GARLIC MAYO: Mince garlic with salt until smooth paste; stir into mayonnaise along with lemon juice and hot pepper sauce. Set aside.

In skillet, fry bacon until crisp; drain on paper towel–lined plate. Drain fat from pan.

Holding knife horizontally, slice each chicken breast through thickest part and open like book; between plastic wrap, pound to even, generous ¼-inch (5 mm) thickness. Sprinkle with salt and pepper. Cook in same skillet over medium-high heat, turning once, until no longer pink inside, 6 to 8 minutes. Transfer to cutting board and slice.

Cut tomato in half lengthwise; slice crosswise. Spread garlic mayo over tortillas. Top with chicken, bacon, lettuce and tomato. Fold in bottom and sides; roll up. Cut in half.

Makes 4 servings. PER SERVING: about 533 cal, 42 g pro, 20 g total fat (6 g sat. fat), 43 g carb, 3 g fibre, 101 mg chol, 1,101 mg sodium, 631 mg potassium. % RDI: 4% calcium, 24% iron, 12% vit A, 12% vit C, 24% folate.

Top & Bottom Crust Pizza

This tasty double-crust pizza freezes well, so you don't have to go and get it (or wait for the delivery guy) when you want a slice. Wrap and freeze wedges for the perfect heat-up-and-dash dinner.

1 tbsp **vegetable oil**

1 **onion,** chopped

2 cloves **garlic,** minced

1 **sweet green pepper,** chopped

¼ tsp each **salt** and **pepper**

1 lb (450 g) **pizza dough**

2 **eggs**

1 cup shredded **mozzarella cheese**
  (see Tip, below)

1 cup shredded **Cheddar cheese**

6 oz (170 g) **salami,** ham or smoked
  turkey, diced

2 tbsp minced **fresh parsley**

1 **egg yolk**

In skillet, heat oil over medium heat; fry onion, garlic, green pepper, salt and pepper until softened, 4 minutes. Let cool.

Meanwhile, on floured surface, roll out half of the dough into 10-inch (25 cm) circle. Place on greased pizza pan or rimless baking sheet. Set aside.

In bowl, whisk eggs; stir in mozzarella and Cheddar cheeses, salami, parsley and onion mixture. Leaving 1-inch (2.5 cm) border around edge, spread over dough on pan.

Roll out remaining dough into 10-inch (25 cm) circle. In bowl, whisk egg yolk with 1 tsp water; lightly brush some over border of bottom crust. Place top crust over filling; with fork, press edge to seal. Brush with remaining egg yolk mixture; cut 3 slits in top crust.

Bake in 375°F (190°C) oven until golden, about 45 minutes. *(Make-ahead: Let cool for 30 minutes. Refrigerate until cold. Wrap whole pizza or individual wedges in plastic wrap and overwrap with heavy-duty foil; freeze for up to 1 month. Thaw in refrigerator. Place on greased baking sheet; bake in 400°F/200°C oven until crisp and hot, about 12 minutes.)*

Makes 6 to 8 servings. PER EACH OF 8 SERVINGS: about 353 cal, 16 g pro, 18 g total fat (8 g sat. fat), 31 g carb, 1 g fibre, 116 mg chol, 733 mg sodium. % RDI: 20% calcium, 16% iron, 12% vit A, 22% vit C, 16% folate.

best
TIPS
ever

If you're shredding a lot of cheese, use the shredder blade of your food processor to make short work of it. Chill the cheese for 20 to 30 minutes before shredding to firm it up.

Oatmeal Chocolate Chip Cookies

Cookies are the ultimate on-the-go treat. These classic oatmeal cookies get dressed up with chocolate chips, but feel free to substitute raisins or dried cranberries if you prefer.

⅔ cup **butter,** softened

1 cup packed **brown sugar**

1 **egg**

2 tsp **vanilla**

1½ cups **large-flake rolled oats**

1 cup **all-purpose flour**

½ tsp each **baking powder** and **baking soda**

¼ tsp **salt**

1½ cups **chocolate chips**

In large bowl, beat butter with brown sugar until fluffy; beat in egg and vanilla. Whisk together oats, flour, baking powder, baking soda and salt; stir into butter mixture until combined. Stir in chocolate chips.

Drop by heaping 1 tbsp, about 2 inches (5 cm) apart, onto parchment paper–lined rimless baking sheets. Bake in top and bottom thirds of 375°F (190°C) oven, rotating and switching pans halfway through, until golden, 12 minutes.

Let cool on pans on racks for 2 minutes. Transfer to racks; let cool. *(Make-ahead: Store in airtight container for up to 5 days or freeze for up to 2 weeks.)*

Makes about 36 cookies. PER COOKIE: about 119 cal, 1 g pro, 6 g total fat (3 g sat. fat), 16 g carb, 1 g fibre, 16 mg chol, 75 mg sodium. % RDI: 1% calcium, 5% iron, 4% vit A, 4% folate.

classic cookies

Peanut Butter Cookies

Another childhood favourite, these chewy, moist cookies are delightful with coffee or tea. And because they're homemade, they are fresher and tastier than any you can get in a coffee shop.

1 cup **butter,** softened (see Tips, below)

¾ cup packed **brown sugar**

¾ cup **granulated sugar**

1 cup **peanut butter** (see Tips, below)

2 **eggs**

1 tsp **vanilla**

2½ cups **all-purpose flour**

1 tsp **baking soda**

1 tsp **baking powder**

¼ tsp **salt**

In large bowl, beat together butter, brown sugar and granulated sugar until fluffy. Beat in peanut butter; beat in eggs, 1 at a time. Beat in vanilla.

Whisk together flour, baking soda, baking powder and salt; stir into butter mixture in 2 additions.

Scoop dough by rounded 1 tbsp; roll into balls. Arrange, 2 inches (5 cm) apart, on rimless baking sheets. Using fork dipped in flour, press balls to make crisscross pattern and flatten to ½-inch (1 cm) thickness.

Bake, 1 sheet at a time, in 350°F (180°C) oven until edges and bottoms are golden, 10 to 12 minutes. Let cool on pan on rack for 2 minutes. Transfer to rack; let cool completely.

Makes 44 cookies. PER COOKIE: about 128 cal, 3 g pro, 8 g total fat (3 g sat. fat), 13 g carb, 1 g fibre, 19 mg chol, 109 mg sodium, 54 mg potassium. % RDI: 1% calcium, 4% iron, 4% vit A, 7% folate.

best
TIPS
ever

- Smooth peanut butter is easier to beat in, but if you like a little nutty crunch in your cookies, use crunchy peanut butter instead.

- Soften butter for an hour or two at room temperature before beating to make cookie dough. Just measure out what you need and set it on a plate on the counter. Keep it out of direct sunlight so it doesn't melt – if it isn't solid when beaten, your cookies will come out thin and overly crisp.

Linzer Cookies
These jam-filled sandwich cookies are based on one of Austria's most famous desserts, the Linzertorte. For soft, chewy cookies, assemble them a day ahead. For crispier cookies, sandwich the same day as serving.

1½ cups **hazelnuts**

2 cups **all-purpose flour**

1½ tsp **cinnamon**

1 tsp **baking powder**

1 tsp grated **lemon zest**

¼ tsp each **ground cloves** and **salt**

1¼ cups **unsalted butter,** softened

¾ cup **granulated sugar**

1 **egg**

1 **egg yolk**

1 tsp **vanilla**

1 cup **raspberry jam**

Icing sugar

On baking sheet, toast hazelnuts in 350°F (180°C) oven until fragrant and skins crack, about 8 minutes. Transfer to tea towel; rub to remove most of the skins.

In food processor, whirl hazelnuts until finely ground. Add flour, cinnamon, baking powder, lemon zest, cloves and salt; pulse to combine.

In large bowl, beat butter with granulated sugar until light and fluffy; beat in egg. Beat in egg yolk, then vanilla. Stir in flour mixture in 2 additions. Divide dough in half; flatten into discs. Wrap each and refrigerate for 1 hour.

On lightly floured surface, roll out each disc to scant ¼-inch (5 mm) thickness. Using 2½-inch (6 cm) round crinkle cookie cutter, cut out shapes, rerolling scraps. Using 1-inch (2.5 cm) round crinkle or star-shaped cutter, cut centres out of half of the cookies to make tops.

Place, about 1 inch (2.5 cm) apart, on parchment paper–lined rimless baking sheets. Bake in 350°F (180°C) oven until golden, about 11 minutes. Let cool on pans on racks.

Spread generous 1 tsp raspberry jam on each cookie bottom. Dust icing sugar over cookie tops; place on jam filling.

Makes about 36 cookies. PER COOKIE: about 162 cal, 2 g pro, 10 g total fat (4 g sat. fat), 17 g carb, 1 g fibre, 28 mg chol, 30 mg sodium, 56 mg potassium. % RDI: 2% calcium, 4% iron, 6% vit A, 2% vit C, 10% folate.

sweet treats

Honey-Caramel Apple Bundt Cake

Be sure to use in-season apples that are firm and sweet-tart. The cake alone is dairy-free. If you're making it for a kosher meal or for someone with a dairy intolerance, drizzle the cake with warmed honey rather than the honey caramel sauce.

¾ cup **light-tasting olive oil**

½ cup **granulated sugar**

½ cup **liquid honey**

3 **eggs**

1 tsp **vanilla**

2 cups **all-purpose flour**

1½ tsp **cinnamon**

1 tsp each **baking powder** and **baking soda**

½ tsp **salt**

3 cups diced peeled **apples**

HONEY CARAMEL:

½ cup **granulated sugar**

¼ cup **mild liquid honey** (such as clover or wildflower)

3 tbsp **whipping cream (35%)**

2 tbsp **butter**

In large bowl, whisk together oil, sugar, honey, eggs and vanilla. Whisk together flour, cinnamon, baking powder, baking soda and salt; stir into egg mixture just until combined. Stir in apples. Scrape into greased 10-inch (3 L) Bundt pan.

Bake in 325°F (160°C) oven until cake tester inserted in centre comes out clean, 40 to 50 minutes. Let cool in pan on rack for 10 minutes; transfer to rack and let cool completely.

HONEY CARAMEL: In heavy saucepan, bring sugar, honey and 2 tbsp water to boil over medium-high heat, brushing down side of pan with pastry brush dipped in cold water. Cook until deep amber colour, about 8 minutes. Remove from heat.

Standing back and averting face, stir in cream and butter. Let cool until caramel is thick enough to coat back of spoon, about 15 minutes. Drizzle warm caramel over cake.

Makes 12 servings. PER SERVING: about 386 cal, 4 g pro, 18 g total fat (4 g sat. fat), 54 g carb, 1 g fibre, 56 mg chol, 258 mg sodium, 80 mg potassium. % RDI: 3% calcium, 10% iron, 5% vit A, 2% vit C, 22% folate.

best honey desserts

Honey-Drenched Phyllo Coil

The combination of perfumed almond paste filling and honey-soaked phyllo makes this stunning coil one of the most beautiful Moroccan pastries.

5 sheets **phyllo pastry**

¼ cup **butter,** melted

½ cup **liquid honey,** warmed

2 tbsp **sliced almonds,** toasted

ALMOND PASTE:

3 cups **blanched almonds**

⅔ cup **granulated sugar**

¾ cup **butter,** softened

2 tbsp **orange flower water** (see Tip, below)

1 tsp **cinnamon**

ALMOND PASTE: In food processor, chop almonds with sugar until powdered. Add butter, orange flower water and cinnamon; pulse until ball forms. Set aside.

Place 1 phyllo sheet on work surface, keeping remainder covered with damp tea towel to prevent drying out. Brush lightly with butter.

Divide almond paste into 5 pieces; roll each into 16-inch (40 cm) long log. Leaving ½-inch (1 cm) borders at ends, place almond paste along 1 long edge of phyllo. Roll up firmly and pinch ends together; brush lightly with butter.

Place roll, seam side down, around edge of greased 9-inch (2.5 L) springform pan. Repeat to make 4 more rolls, fitting each into pan to make spiral and cover bottom.

Bake in 400°F (200°C) oven until crispy and golden, about 10 minutes. Brush immediately with warm honey; let cool in pan on rack for 15 minutes. *(Make-ahead: Let cool completely. Cover with plastic wrap and let stand for up to 48 hours.)* Garnish with almonds.

Makes 8 servings. PER SERVING: about 720 cal, 14 g pro, 54 g total fat (17 g sat. fat), 54 g carb, 6 g fibre, 73 mg chol, 326 mg sodium. % RDI: 13% calcium, 21% iron, 22% vit A, 14% folate.

best **TIPS** ever

Look for bottles of perfumy orange flower water in the baking aisle of some larger supermarkets. Or try Middle Eastern grocery stores – it's usually beside the rose water.

Honey Cream With Vanilla-Roasted Figs

Honey is the star here, so use a flavourful variety such as clover or orange blossom. Thyme may seem like an unusual addition, but floral honey and grassy thyme are perfect partners.

2 tbsp packed **brown sugar**

1 tbsp **liquid honey**

1 tsp **vanilla**

½ tsp chopped **fresh thyme**

½ tsp grated **lemon zest**

Pinch **salt**

1 lb (450 g) **fresh figs** (such as Black Mission), about 9 (see Tip, below)

HONEY CREAM:

2 cups **whipping cream (35%)**

4 **egg yolks**

⅓ cup **clover honey** or other flavourful honey

HONEY CREAM: In heatproof bowl, whisk together 1 cup of the cream, egg yolks and honey. Set bowl over saucepan of simmering water; cook, stirring, until mixture is thick enough to coat back of spoon, about 15 minutes. Strain through fine sieve into large bowl. Place plastic wrap directly on surface; let cool. Refrigerate until cold, about 1 hour.

Whip remaining cream; fold into honey mixture. Refrigerate until cold and mixture is thick enough to mound on spoon, 3½ to 4 hours.

Meanwhile, in bowl, stir together brown sugar, honey, vanilla, thyme, lemon zest and salt. Cut figs in half lengthwise and add to bowl; toss to coat. Scrape into 8-inch (2 L) square baking dish; turn figs cut side down. Cover with foil.

Bake in 400°F (200°C) oven until fork-tender, 20 to 25 minutes. Let cool in pan on rack until liquid is reabsorbed, about 20 minutes. Serve warm or at room temperature with honey cream.

Makes 6 servings. PER SERVING: about 442 cal, 4 g pro, 32 g total fat (19 g sat. fat), 40 g carb, 3 g fibre, 238 mg chol, 37 mg sodium, 280 mg potassium. % RDI: 9% calcium, 6% iron, 31% vit A, 3% vit C, 10% folate.

best TIPS ever

Fresh figs should be slightly soft but not mushy. Avoid bruised or hard fruit and look for firm stems – if the stem doesn't jiggle, the fruit inside should be ripe but not overripe.

Rhubarb Banana Crumble

If fresh rhubarb isn't in season, thaw frozen rhubarb in a colander in the sink to drain off excess liquid. Measure it after it's thawed to get the proper amount – the pieces shrink a little as they lose moisture.

5 cups sliced **fresh rhubarb**

⅓ cup **granulated sugar**

2 tbsp **all-purpose flour**

3 **bananas,** chopped

TOPPING:

¾ cup **quick-cooking rolled oats** (not instant)

⅓ cup **all-purpose flour**

¼ cup each **granulated sugar** and packed **brown sugar**

¼ tsp **cinnamon**

⅓ cup cold **unsalted butter,** cubed

¼ cup **walnut pieces**

¼ cup **pine nuts** (optional)

Toss together rhubarb, sugar and flour; divide among 8 greased 3½- x 1½-inch (175 mL) ramekins or pour into greased 8-inch (2 L) square baking dish. Cover with foil; bake in 400°F (200°C) oven, stirring once, until tender-crisp, about 25 minutes. Arrange bananas over top.

TOPPING: Meanwhile, in bowl, combine oats, flour, granulated sugar, brown sugar and cinnamon; with fingers, blend in butter until crumbly. Mix in walnuts, and pine nuts (if using). Scatter over bananas, pressing gently.

Bake, uncovered, in 350°F (180°C) oven until filling is bubbly and crumble is golden, about 25 minutes.

Makes 8 servings. PER SERVING: about 291 cal, 4 g pro, 11 g total fat (5 g sat. fat), 48 g carb, 4 g fibre, 20 mg chol, 7 mg sodium, 332 mg potassium. % RDI: 17% calcium, 10% iron, 8% vit A, 10% vit C, 13% folate.

easy weeknight desserts

Warm Berry Shortcake
Dessert on the grill is an unexpected delight, and this one proves how amazingly tasty it can be. In late summer, try this shortcake with juicy sliced fresh peaches instead of the berries.

2 cups halved **fresh strawberries**

1 cup **fresh raspberries**

½ cup **fresh blueberries**

2 tbsp **granulated sugar**

2 tsp **cornstarch**

1 tsp **lemon juice**

4 slices (½ inch/1 cm thick each) **pound cake**

4 scoops **vanilla ice cream** (about 2 cups)

Cut 4-foot (1.2 m) piece heavy-duty foil; fold in half. Arrange strawberries, raspberries and blueberries on 1 side close to centre.

Combine sugar and cornstarch; sprinkle over fruit. Sprinkle with lemon juice; gently toss. Fold foil over and seal to form packet. *(Make-ahead: Refrigerate for up to 2 hours.)*

Place on grill over medium heat; close lid and grill, turning once, until hot and juices are thickened, about 10 minutes. Let stand for 10 minutes.

Grill cake, turning once, until grill-marked, about 6 minutes. Arrange on dessert plates. Top each with scoop of ice cream. Spoon berry mixture over top.

Makes 4 servings. PER SERVING: about 360 cal, 5 g pro, 15 g total fat (6 g sat. fat), 55 g carb, 4 g fibre, 51 mg chol, 205 mg sodium. % RDI: 12% calcium, 9% iron, 10% vit A, 70% vit C, 14% folate.

Butterscotch Pudding

The longer you cook the brown sugar and butter in this old-fashioned dessert, the richer the butterscotch flavour.

⅓ cup **unsalted butter**

⅔ cup packed **brown sugar**

½ cup **whipping cream (35%)**

1¾ cups **homogenized milk**

2 **egg yolks**

Pinch **salt**

¼ cup **cornstarch**

In saucepan, melt butter over medium-low heat; stir in brown sugar until dissolved and bubbling. Boil, stirring occasionally, until light molasses to coffee colour, 3 to 6 minutes. Whisk in cream; whisk until mixture is liquefied, about 1 minute.

Whisk together 1½ cups of the milk, egg yolks and salt; whisk into sugar mixture and cook over medium heat, stirring occasionally, for 6 minutes.

Whisk cornstarch with remaining milk; whisk into sugar mixture and cook, whisking constantly, until thickened, about 1 minute. Transfer to bowl. Place plastic wrap directly on surface (see Tip, below); let cool to room temperature. *(Make-ahead: Refrigerate for up to 24 hours. Serve at room temperature.)*

Makes 4 to 6 servings. PER EACH OF 6 SERVINGS: about 332 cal, 4 g pro, 21 g total fat (13 g sat. fat), 33 g carb, 0 g fibre, 130 mg chol, 56 mg sodium, 218 mg potassium. % RDI: 12% calcium, 5% iron, 20% vit A, 6% folate.

Chocolate Peanut Butter Pudding Cake

Tempt your taste buds with this classic combo in cake form – it's so addictive!

¾ cup **all-purpose flour**

⅓ cup **granulated sugar**

1 tsp **baking powder**

⅓ cup **milk**

1 **egg,** beaten

3 tbsp **natural peanut butter**

¾ cup packed **brown sugar**

¼ cup **cocoa powder**

1 cup **boiling water**

In large bowl, whisk together flour, granulated sugar and baking powder. Whisk together milk, egg and peanut butter; stir into flour mixture. Scrape into greased 8-inch (2 L) square baking dish.

In heatproof bowl, whisk brown sugar with cocoa powder; whisk in boiling water until smooth. Pour over cake; do not stir. Bake in 350°F (180°C) oven until cake is firm to the touch, 30 minutes. Let cool in pan on rack for 10 minutes.

Makes 4 to 6 servings. PER EACH OF 6 SERVINGS: about 281 cal, 6 g pro, 6 g total fat (1 g sat. fat), 54 g carb, 2 g fibre, 32 mg chol, 81 mg sodium. % RDI: 7% calcium, 16% iron, 2% vit A, 17% folate.

change it up

Slow Cooker Chocolate Peanut Butter Pudding Cake: Scrape batter into greased slow cooker. Pour cocoa mixture over top; do not stir. Cover and cook on high until cake is firm to the touch, about 2 hours.

best **TIPS** ever

Placing plastic wrap directly on the surface of a pudding as it cools keeps condensation from forming and dripping onto it. No one likes a watery pudding!

Caramel Coconut Blondies

The gooey caramel topping for these blondies is so easy – all you need are soft caramels and water. Look for these individually wrapped sweets in bulk food stores or in bags in the candy aisle.

½ cup **unsalted butter**

1¼ cups packed **brown sugar**

2 **eggs**

1 tsp **vanilla**

1¼ cups **all-purpose flour**

½ cup **sweetened shredded coconut**

½ tsp **baking powder**

¼ tsp **salt**

CARAMEL TOPPING:

10 **caramel candies**

In large bowl, beat butter with brown sugar until light and fluffy. Beat in eggs, 1 at a time; beat in vanilla.

Whisk together flour, coconut, baking powder and salt; stir into butter mixture. Spread in parchment paper–lined 8-inch (2 L) square cake pan.

Bake in 325°F (160°C) oven until cake tester inserted in centre comes out with a few crumbs clinging, about 35 minutes. Let cool in pan on rack.

CARAMEL TOPPING: In saucepan, melt caramels with 2 tbsp water over medium-low heat until smooth. Drizzle over cooled blondies. Refrigerate for 20 minutes. *(Make-ahead: Wrap in plastic wrap and store for up to 24 hours.)*

Cut blondies into squares.

Makes 16 pieces. PER PIECE: about 194 cal, 2 g pro, 8 g total fat (5 g sat. fat), 30 g carb, trace fibre, 39 mg chol, 81 mg sodium, 101 mg potassium. % RDI: 3% calcium, 6% iron, 6% vit A, 11% folate.

Sweet Cherry Custard Tart

Fresh cherries are so wonderful – and in season for such a short time – that it's hard to get past just eating them out of hand. But you can with this French tart, which highlights the fruit in a chic way.

1 cup **all-purpose flour**

½ cup **butter,** softened

1 **egg yolk**

1 tbsp **granulated sugar**

Pinch **salt**

FILLING:

2 cups pitted **sweet cherries** (see Tip, below)

2 **eggs,** beaten

½ cup **whipping cream (35%)**

¼ cup **all-purpose flour**

¼ cup **granulated sugar**

1 tbsp grated **lemon zest**

1 tbsp **vanilla**

Pinch **salt**

Place flour in bowl; make well in centre. Add butter, egg yolk, sugar and salt; mix with fork until egg mixture is smooth. Gradually stir in flour to make soft ragged dough. Press into disc; wrap and refrigerate for 1 hour.

Between waxed paper, roll out pastry into 11-inch (28 cm) circle. Peel off top paper; invert pastry and fit into 9-inch (23 cm) tart pan with removable bottom. Trim to leave 1-inch (2.5 cm) overhang; fold inside rim and press pastry together. Place pan on rimmed baking sheet.

FILLING: Sprinkle cherries over pastry. Whisk together eggs, cream, flour, sugar, lemon zest, vanilla and salt; pour over cherries. Bake on bottom rack in 375°F (190°C) oven until golden and tip of knife inserted into custard comes out clean, about 45 minutes. Let cool in pan on rack.

Makes 12 servings. PER SERVING: about 207 cal, 3 g pro, 13 g total fat (7 g sat. fat), 20 g carb, 1 g fibre, 88 mg chol, 93 mg sodium. % RDI: 2% calcium, 6% iron, 13% vit A, 3% vit C, 4% folate.

best TIPS ever

If you choose to make this tart outside of cherry season, you can use frozen cherries, but make sure they're individually quick frozen ones that are plump. Thaw them in a colander in the sink to remove excess water, then measure them to get the proper volume. They will create pink streaks in the custard, so try to move them as little as possible when pouring it in.

Milk Chocolate Cupcakes

With two types of chocolate, these treats will appeal to every chocoholic.

2 oz (60 g) **semisweet chocolate,** chopped

1 oz (30 g) **milk chocolate,** chopped

½ cup **butter,** softened

½ cup **granulated sugar**

2 **eggs**

1 tsp **vanilla**

¾ cup **all-purpose flour**

½ tsp **baking powder**

½ tsp **baking soda**

¼ tsp **salt**

½ cup **sour cream**

In bowl over saucepan of hot (not boiling) water, melt semisweet chocolate and milk chocolate; let cool to room temperature.

In large bowl, beat butter with sugar until fluffy; beat in eggs, 1 at a time. Beat in vanilla and chocolate.

Whisk together flour, baking powder, baking soda and salt; stir into butter mixture alternately with sour cream, making 3 additions of dry ingredients and 2 of sour cream. Spoon into paper-lined or greased muffin cups.

Bake in 350°F (180°C) oven until cake tester inserted in centre comes out clean, 20 to 25 minutes. Transfer to rack; let cool.

Makes 12 cupcakes. PER CUPCAKE: about 192 cal, 3 g pro, 12 g total fat (7 g sat. fat), 19 g carb, 1 g fibre, 56 mg chol, 184 mg sodium, 59 mg potassium. % RDI: 3% calcium, 4% iron, 9% vit A, 10% folate.

Smooth Chocolate Glaze

This warm, not-too-sweet silky chocolate glaze is the ultimate cupcake topper.

3 oz (90 g) **bittersweet chocolate,** chopped

1 tbsp **butter**

⅓ cup **whipping cream (35%)**

Place chocolate and butter in heatproof bowl. In saucepan, heat cream just until boiling; pour over chocolate mixture, whisking until smooth. Let cool slightly, about 10 minutes.

Makes about ⅔ cup, enough for 12 cupcakes. PER CUPCAKE: about 70 cal, 1 g pro, 6 g total fat (4 g sat. fat), 4 g carb, 1 g fibre, 11 mg chol, 9 mg sodium, 6 mg potassium. % RDI: 1% calcium, 2% iron, 3% vit A.

change it up

Chilled Chocolate Spread: Refrigerate glaze until thickened but not firm, 15 to 20 minutes. Spread over cupcakes like icing.

Molten Chocolate Cakes

Each of these dramatic mini cakes has a truffle in the middle. As it bakes, the truffle melts, ready to flow at the first stab of a spoon. Try different liqueurs in the truffles and crème anglaise for new flavour twists.

¾ cup **butter,** softened

1 cup **granulated sugar** (approx)

12 oz (375 g) **bittersweet chocolate,**
   chopped

4 **eggs**

4 **egg yolks**

1 tbsp **vanilla**

1 cup **all-purpose flour**

TRUFFLES:

4 oz (125 g) **bittersweet chocolate,**
   chopped

⅓ cup **whipping cream (35%)**

2 tbsp **Irish cream liqueur**
   (or 1 tsp vanilla)

CRÈME ANGLAISE:

1 cup **18% cream** or whipping
   cream (35%)

1 cup **milk**

¼ cup **granulated sugar**

6 **egg yolks**

1 tsp **cornstarch**

2 tbsp **Irish cream liqueur**
   (or 1 tsp vanilla)

1 tsp **vanilla**

CRÈME ANGLAISE: In heavy saucepan, heat cream, milk and half of the sugar over medium heat until bubbles form around edge. Meanwhile, in bowl, whisk egg yolks, cornstarch and remaining sugar; whisk in hot cream in thin stream. Return to pan; cook over medium-low heat, stirring constantly and without simmering, until thick enough to coat spoon, 3 to 5 minutes. Strain into clean bowl. Stir in liqueur and vanilla. Place plastic wrap directly on surface; let cool. Refrigerate until cold, 1 hour. *(Make-ahead: Refrigerate for up to 3 days.)*

TRUFFLES: Line rimmed baking sheet with plastic wrap; set aside. Place chocolate in heatproof bowl. In saucepan, heat cream over medium heat until steaming. Pour over chocolate; whisk until smooth. Whisk in liqueur; refrigerate until firm, 1 hour. Spoon in 8 mounds onto prepared baking sheet. Roll into balls. Cover and freeze until firm, about 4 hours. *(Make-ahead: Freeze in airtight container for up to 1 week.)*

Grease eight 3½- x 1½-inch (175 mL) ramekins with no more than 1 tbsp of the butter. Line bottoms with parchment paper; sprinkle scant 1 tsp of the sugar inside each. Set aside. In bowl over saucepan of hot (not boiling) water, melt chocolate with remaining butter. Let cool to room temperature. In separate bowl, beat eggs, egg yolks and remaining sugar until thickened, about 5 minutes. Fold in chocolate mixture and vanilla. Stir in flour. Spoon half into prepared cups; place frozen truffle in centre of each. Spoon remaining batter over top. *(Make-ahead: Cover and refrigerate for up to 24 hours.)*

Bake on rimmed baking sheet in 350°F (180°C) oven until centres are sunken, soft and shiny, 22 minutes. Let cool for 2 minutes. With knife, gently loosen edges. Unmould onto plates; peel off paper. Serve immediately with crème anglaise.

Makes 8 servings. PER SERVING: about 890 cal, 17 g pro, 69 g total fat (39 g sat. fat), 71 g carb, 9 g fibre, 436 mg chol, 262 mg sodium. % RDI: 15% calcium, 39% iron, 41% vit A, 32% folate.

decadent desserts

Spiced Pecan Bourbon Tart
A twist on classic pecan pie, this tart has an easy pat-in crust and is lip-smackingly good with or without the bourbon. Serve with whipped cream.

3 **eggs**

1 cup packed **brown sugar**

½ cup **corn syrup** (approx),
  see Tip, below

¼ cup **bourbon** or rye whisky

2 tbsp **butter,** melted

½ tsp **cinnamon**

¼ tsp each **ground nutmeg, ground
  cloves** and **ground allspice**

1½ cups **pecan halves**

2 tbsp **corn syrup,** warmed

PAT-IN PASTRY:

1¼ cups **all-purpose flour**

2 tbsp **granulated sugar**

¼ tsp **salt**

⅓ cup cold **butter,** cubed

2 tbsp cold **water**

1 tsp **vinegar**

PAT-IN PASTRY: In food processor, mix together flour, sugar and salt. Pulse in butter until in fine crumbs. Add water and vinegar; pulse 2 or 3 times or until blended but still crumbly. Squeeze together in small handfuls and pat evenly and firmly over bottom and up side of 9-inch (23 cm) tart pan with removable bottom. Refrigerate for 15 minutes. *(Make-ahead: Cover and refrigerate for up to 24 hours.)*

In bowl, whisk together eggs, brown sugar, corn syrup, bourbon, butter, cinnamon, nutmeg, cloves and allspice; stir in pecans. Scrape filling into prepared tart shell.

Bake on bottom rack in 375°F (190°C) oven, shielding edge with foil if browning too much, until pastry is golden and filling is just firm to the touch, about 45 minutes. Brush filling with more corn syrup; let cool. *(Make-ahead: Cover with foil and let stand at room temperature for up to 1 day.)*

Using serrated knife, cut into wedges.

Makes 12 servings. PER SERVING: about 347 cal, 4 g pro, 18 g total fat (6 g sat. fat), 46 g carb, 1 g fibre, 65 mg chol, 161 mg sodium. % RDI: 3% calcium, 10% iron, 9% vit A, 12% folate.

change it up
Spiced Pecan Tart: Omit bourbon. Decrease brown sugar to ¾ cup and increase corn syrup to ¾ cup.

best **TIPS** ever

Corn syrup comes in various colours. In Canada, it can be golden or white; in the United States, there's also a dark (brown) version. The darker the colour, the more molasses-type flavour the syrup will have. But all corn syrup behaves the same way in cooking and baking, so you can usually use the different colours interchangeably.

Cherry Cheesecake

This retro dessert gets an update with a homemade cherry topping instead of the typical canned variety. Serve it right from the fridge so the squares are easy to cut.

2 cups **graham wafer crumbs**

⅓ cup **butter,** melted

FILLING:

2 pkg (250 g each) **cream cheese,** softened

1 can (300 mL) **sweetened condensed milk**

¼ cup **whipping cream (35%)**

½ tsp **vanilla**

TOPPING:

1 jar (28 oz/796 mL) **red sour cherries in light syrup**

¼ cup **granulated sugar**

1 tbsp **cornstarch**

½ tsp grated **orange zest**

In bowl, stir crumbs with butter until moistened; press into greased 13- x 9-inch (3 L) baking dish. Bake in 350°F (180°C) oven until set, about 10 minutes. Let cool in pan on rack.

FILLING: In large bowl, beat cream cheese until fluffy; beat in sweetened condensed milk, cream and vanilla. Pour over base, smoothing top. Cover and refrigerate until firm, about 4 hours.

TOPPING: Reserving juice in saucepan, drain cherries; add sugar to juice. Bring to boil. Whisk cornstarch with 1 tbsp cold water; whisk into juice mixture and cook, stirring, until thickened, about 1 minute. Remove from heat. Stir in cherries and orange zest; let cool. *(Make-ahead: Cover and refrigerate cheesecake and topping separately for up to 2 days.)*

Cut cheesecake crosswise into quarters, then lengthwise into thirds; serve each square topped with dollop of topping.

Makes 12 servings. PER SERVING: about 459 cal, 8 g pro, 26 g total fat (16 g sat. fat), 51 g carb, 1 g fibre, 77 mg chol, 317 mg sodium. % RDI: 13% calcium, 16% iron, 30% vit A, 3% vit C, 12% folate.

Rhubarb Black Raspberry Galettes

These rustic individual pies can be made with your choice of berries; just use the ripest local ones you can find. Cornmeal makes the crust crispy – it's best the same day it's baked.

2 cups **all-purpose flour**

½ cup **cornmeal**

1 tbsp **granulated sugar**

½ tsp **salt**

1 cup cold **unsalted butter,** cubed

3 tbsp **sour cream**

½ cup **ice water** (approx)

FILLING:

1 cup **granulated sugar**

3 tbsp **cornstarch**

5 cups sliced **fresh rhubarb**

1½ cups **fresh black raspberries** or
     fresh red raspberries

1 tbsp **lemon juice**

⅓ cup **dried bread crumbs**

2 tbsp **butter,** softened

GLAZE:

1 **egg yolk**

In bowl, mix flour, cornmeal, sugar and salt; using pastry blender, cut in butter until in large crumbs. In glass measure, whisk sour cream with ice water; drizzle over flour mixture, tossing with fork until dough comes together and adding up to 1 tbsp more water if necessary. Divide into 6 pieces; shape into discs. Wrap each in plastic wrap; refrigerate until chilled, 30 minutes. *(Make-ahead: Refrigerate for up to 24 hours.)*

FILLING: Remove 2 tbsp of the sugar and set aside for sprinkling over galettes. Whisk remaining sugar with cornstarch. In large bowl, toss together rhubarb, raspberries, lemon juice and cornstarch mixture.

On floured surface, roll out each disc of pastry into 8½-inch (21 cm) circle, leaving edge ragged. Arrange 3 circles each on 2 parchment paper–lined large rimmed baking sheets.

Sprinkle centre of each circle with bread crumbs. Spoon 1 cup rhubarb mixture over top of each; dot each with 1 tsp butter. Lift pastry up and over filling to form about 5-inch (12 cm) circle, letting pastry fall naturally into folds around edge and leaving centre uncovered. *(Make-ahead: Cover and refrigerate for up to 24 hours.)*

GLAZE: Beat egg yolk with 1 tbsp water; brush over pastry. Sprinkle with reserved sugar.

Bake on top and bottom racks in 425°F (220°C) oven for 10 minutes. Reduce heat to 350°F (180°C); bake for 10 minutes. Switch and rotate pans. Bake until filling is bubbly and crust is golden, about 15 minutes. Let cool on pan on rack for 15 minutes.

Makes 6 servings. PER SERVING: about 733 cal, 8 g pro, 37 g total fat (23 g sat. fat), 93 g carb, 5 g fibre, 128 mg chol, 277 mg sodium. % RDI: 12% calcium, 21% iron, 35% vit A, 24% vit C, 60% folate.

fresh & fruity desserts

Roasted Summer Fruit
With Spiced Mascarpone Cream Fruit and cream is a classic
dessert pairing. Here, the fruit develops a rich, caramelized taste as it roasts.

⅓ cup **sliced almonds**

2 each **apricots** and **plums,**
   quartered

2 **peaches** or nectarines, quartered

⅓ cup packed **brown sugar**

3 tbsp **brandy** or apple juice

2 tbsp **butter,** melted

1 cup **mascarpone cheese**

½ tsp **vanilla**

½ tsp **ground ginger**

Pinch **ground cardamom** (optional)

½ cup **whipping cream (35%)**

In dry skillet over medium heat, toast almonds, shaking pan often, until light golden, about 5 minutes. Transfer to plate and let cool.

In small roasting pan or large ovenproof skillet, toss together apricots, plums, peaches, half of the brown sugar, the brandy and butter. Roast in 400°F (200°C) oven, stirring occasionally, until fork-tender, 15 to 20 minutes.

Meanwhile, in bowl, beat together mascarpone cheese, remaining brown sugar, vanilla, ginger, and cardamom (if using) until smooth. In separate bowl, whip cream; fold half into cheese mixture. Fold in remaining cream and half of the almonds. *(Make-ahead: Cover and refrigerate fruit and cream separately for up to 4 hours.)*

Mound cheese mixture in bowls or dessert dishes. Spoon fruit and pan juices over top. Sprinkle with remaining almonds.

Makes 4 servings. PER SERVING: about 580 cal, 6 g pro, 47 g total fat (27 g sat. fat), 34 g carb, 3 g fibre, 137 mg chol, 76 mg sodium, 378 mg potassium. % RDI: 10% calcium, 7% iron, 38% vit A, 10% vit C, 3% folate.

Melon With Citrus Blueberry Sauce Summer means fresh berries, melons and mint from the garden, and this dessert highlights them all.

Half **cantaloupe** or honeydew melon
   (see Tip, below)
1 **pink grapefruit**
1 tbsp each **lemon juice** and
   liquid honey
Pinch **hot pepper flakes** (optional)
½ cup **fresh blueberries**
2 tsp shredded **fresh mint leaves**

Seed cantaloupe; cut into 8 wedges. Cut off skin. Set aside.

Cut off peel, pith and outer membranes of grapefruit. Working over bowl to catch juices, cut between membranes and fruit to release segments into bowl; squeeze membranes to extract juice.

Arrange melon and grapefruit on plates.

Remove all but 2 tbsp of the grapefruit juice from bowl and reserve to drink. Whisk lemon juice, honey, and hot pepper flakes (if using) into remaining juice in bowl. Stir in blueberries and half of the mint; spoon over fruit. Sprinkle with remaining mint.

Makes 4 servings. PER SERVING: about 69 cal, 1 g pro, trace total fat (0 g sat. fat), 17 g carb, 2 g fibre, 0 mg chol, 8 mg sodium. % RDI: 2% calcium, 2% iron, 23% vit A, 92% vit C, 10% folate.

best
TIPS
ever

Local melons often have better flavour than imported ones because they're picked when they're riper. Look for melons that seem heavy for their size. Take a sniff – if you smell a heavenly aroma, the flesh inside should be ripe.

Tunnel of Peanuts Cake
Natural peanut butter with no added sugar is our choice for this cake, which is particularly delectable thanks to its hidden streusel centre of roasted peanuts, brown sugar and butter.

1 cup **butter,** softened

¾ cup packed **brown sugar**

¾ cup **granulated sugar**

1 cup **natural peanut butter**

3 **eggs**

1 tsp **vanilla**

2½ cups **all-purpose flour**

1 tsp each **baking powder** and **baking soda**

½ tsp **salt**

1½ cups **milk**

PEANUT STREUSEL:

1 cup finely chopped **unsalted roasted peanuts**

⅓ cup packed **brown sugar**

2 tbsp **butter,** melted

GLAZE:

¾ cup **icing sugar**

2 tbsp **milk**

2 tbsp chopped **unsalted roasted peanuts**

Grease 10-cup (2.5 L) fancy or classic Bundt or tube pan; dust with flour. Set aside.

PEANUT STREUSEL: Combine peanuts, brown sugar and butter; set aside.

In large bowl, beat butter with brown and granulated sugars until fluffy; beat in peanut butter. Beat in eggs, 1 at a time, beating well after each; beat in vanilla. Whisk together flour, baking powder, baking soda and salt; stir into butter mixture alternately with milk, making 3 additions of dry ingredients and 2 of milk.

Spoon half of the batter into prepared pan. Make tunnel, about 2 inches (5 cm) wide, in batter. Spoon peanut streusel into tunnel, pressing lightly. Spoon remaining batter over streusel; tap pan on counter and smooth top.

Bake in 325°F (160°C) oven until cake tester inserted in centre comes out clean, about 55 minutes. Let cool in pan on rack for 10 minutes. Turn cake out onto rack; let cool completely. *(Make-ahead: Wrap in plastic wrap; store in airtight container for up to 24 hours or freeze for up to 1 month.)*

GLAZE: Whisk icing sugar with milk; drizzle over cooled cake. Sprinkle peanuts over glaze.

Makes 16 servings. PER SERVING: about 471 cal, 11 g pro, 27 g total fat (10 g sat. fat), 50 g carb, 2 g fibre, 78 mg chol, 324 mg sodium. % RDI: 8% calcium, 15% iron, 15% vit A, 20% folate.

peanut butter desserts

Peanut Butter Fudge

A favourite childhood flavour transforms into a smooth, dense, creamy treat. This fudge makes a gift that's guaranteed to please.

1 pkg (10 oz/300 g) **peanut butter chips**

⅔ cup **sweetened condensed milk**
 (see Tip, below)

¼ cup **whipping cream (35%)**

In heatproof bowl over saucepan of hot (not boiling) water, melt together peanut butter chips, sweetened condensed milk and cream until smooth. Spread in parchment paper–lined 9- x 5-inch (2 L) loaf pan; cover and refrigerate until chilled, about 6 hours.

Cut into 1-inch (2.5 cm) cubes. *(Make-ahead: Refrigerate in airtight container for up to 1 week.)*

Makes 1 lb (450 g), or 32 pieces. PER PIECE: about 71 cal, 2 g pro, 4 g total fat (2 g sat. fat), 8 g carb, trace fibre, 5 mg chol, 31 mg sodium. % RDI: 3% calcium, 1% iron, 1% vit A.

change it up

Peanut Butter & Jelly Fudge: After spreading in loaf pan, drop ¼ cup grape jelly by teaspoonfuls over top; swirl with tip of knife.

best TIPS ever

You'll have some sweetened condensed milk left over after making this fudge. Use it up by treating yourself to a Vietnamese iced coffee or tea. Brew a stronger-than-normal cuppa and pour some of the condensed milk over ice in a tall glass. Add the coffee or tea and stir. Delicious!

Frozen Peanut Butter Pie

Nostalgic for peanut butter and hungry for chocolate? Here they are in a no-bake pie that lives up to your fondest memories.

1 cup **chocolate wafer crumbs**

¼ cup **butter,** melted

FILLING:

⅔ cup **sour cream**

3 tbsp **icing sugar**

2 tbsp **whipping cream (35%)**

⅔ cup **smooth peanut butter**

TOPPING:

2 oz (60 g) **semisweet chocolate,** coarsely chopped

¼ cup **whipping cream (35%)**

¼ cup chopped **unsalted roasted peanuts**

In bowl, stir crumbs with butter until well moistened; pat onto bottom only of 9-inch (23 cm) pie plate. Freeze for 20 minutes.

FILLING: In bowl, whisk together sour cream, icing sugar and whipping cream; whisk in peanut butter until smooth. Spread evenly over crust; freeze for 1 hour.

TOPPING: Meanwhile, in small saucepan, melt chocolate with cream over medium-low heat, stirring until smooth. Let cool for 15 minutes.

Spread chocolate mixture evenly over filling. Sprinkle peanuts around edge of pie. Freeze until completely set, about 1 hour. (*Make-ahead: Wrap in foil and freeze for up to 1 week.*)

Let stand at room temperature for 10 minutes before cutting into wedges.

Makes 12 servings. PER SERVING: about 252 cal, 6 g pro, 20 g total fat (8 g sat. fat), 16 g carb, 2 g fibre, 24 mg chol, 160 mg sodium, 183 mg potassium. % RDI: 3% calcium, 6% iron, 8% vit A, 10% folate.

Strawberry Cheesecake Turnovers

Crisp on the outside and creamy in the middle, these flaky turnovers are a cinch to make. The combination of strawberries and vanilla-scented cheese is heavenly.

1½ cups quartered hulled **fresh strawberries**

4 tsp **granulated sugar**

2 tsp **cornstarch**

1 tsp **lemon juice**

Pinch **cinnamon**

1 pkg (450 g) **frozen butter puff pastry,** thawed

1 **egg**

1 tbsp **Demerara sugar** or granulated sugar

CREAM CHEESE FILLING:

6 oz (170 g) **cream cheese,** softened

⅓ cup **icing sugar**

½ tsp **vanilla**

In small saucepan, stir together strawberries, granulated sugar, cornstarch, lemon juice and cinnamon; let stand for 30 minutes.

Stir 3 tbsp water into strawberry mixture; bring to boil over medium heat. Reduce heat and simmer until thickened and strawberries begin to soften, about 2 minutes. Transfer to bowl; let cool.

CREAM CHEESE FILLING: Meanwhile, beat together cream cheese, icing sugar and vanilla until smooth. Set aside.

On lightly floured surface, roll out each piece of puff pastry into 12-inch (30 cm) square. Cut each into 4 squares.

Spoon some of the cream cheese filling onto half of each square, mounding filling. Top with some of the strawberry mixture. Brush pastry edges with water; fold 1 corner over filling to make triangle. With tines of fork, press edges to seal; pierce top of each turnover in 3 places to make steam vents. Transfer to parchment paper–lined rimmed baking sheets. Refrigerate for 30 minutes. *(Make-ahead: Refrigerate for up to 12 hours. Or layer between waxed paper and freeze in airtight container for up to 2 weeks; bake from frozen, adding 3 minutes to baking time.)*

Whisk egg with 1 tsp water; brush over turnovers. Sprinkle with Demerara sugar. Bake, 1 sheet at a time, in 425°F (220°C) oven until puffed and golden, 15 to 18 minutes. Serve warm or at room temperature.

Makes 8 servings. PER SERVING: about 352 cal, 6 g pro, 22 g total fat (11 g sat. fat), 35 g carb, 2 g fibre, 69 mg chol, 250 mg sodium, 84 mg potassium. % RDI: 2% calcium, 15% iron, 15% vit A, 20% vit C, 4% folate.

easy baked treats

Chocolate Snacking Cake
This dark, moist cake does not call for the two eggs and ½ cup butter of a typical quick cake recipe, but it still tastes utterly decadent.

1⅓ cups **all-purpose flour**

½ cup **cocoa powder**

1 tsp **baking powder**

1 tsp **baking soda**

½ tsp **salt**

1 cup packed **brown sugar**

½ cup **buttermilk**

¼ cup **vegetable oil**

1½ tsp **vanilla**

Icing sugar (optional)

In large bowl, sift together flour, cocoa powder, baking powder, baking soda and salt. Press brown sugar through sieve to remove lumps; combine with dry ingredients. Add buttermilk, ½ cup water, oil and vanilla; whisk until smooth. Scrape into greased 9-inch (2.5 L) square cake pan.

Bake in 350°F (180°C) oven until cake tester inserted in centre comes out clean, about 35 minutes. Let cool completely. Dust with icing sugar (if using). Cut into squares.

Makes 20 servings. PER SERVING: about 105 cal, 2 g pro, 3 g total fat (1 g sat. fat), 18 g carb, 1 g fibre, 0 mg chol, 144 mg sodium, 88 mg potassium. % RDI: 3% calcium, 6% iron, 6% folate.

Tropical Coconut Macaroons Chewy coconut cookies just get better with the addition of candied tropical fruit.

⅔ cup **sweetened condensed milk**

1 **egg white**

Pinch **salt**

2½ cups **unsweetened shredded coconut**
  (see Tips, below)

½ cup slivered **candied pineapple**

½ cup slivered **candied mango** or
  candied papaya

In bowl, whisk together condensed milk, egg white and salt; stir in coconut, pineapple and mango until evenly coated. Drop by rounded 1 tsp onto parchment paper–lined rimless baking sheets.

Bake in 325°F (160°C) oven until golden and no longer sticky to the touch, 15 to 20 minutes. Let cool on pans on racks for 5 minutes. Transfer to racks; let cool.

Makes 50 cookies. PER COOKIE: about 55 cal, 1 g pro, 3 g total fat (3 g sat. fat), 6 g carb, 0 g fibre, 1 mg chol, 8 mg sodium. % RDI: 1% calcium, 1% iron, 3% vit C.

change it up
Tropical Coconut Macaroons With White Chocolate: Dip macaroons into melted white chocolate to coat bottom or half of each.

Ginger Coconut Macaroons: Add ¼ cup chopped crystallized ginger to batter.

Butterscotch Crunch Bars These sweet treats are a quick-to-make contribution to a bake sale – or your cookie jar.

28 **graham crackers**

1 cup **unsalted butter**

1 cup packed **brown sugar**

1½ cups **sliced almonds,** toasted

Lightly grease 15- x 10-inch (38 x 25 cm) rimmed baking sheet; arrange graham crackers on pan. Set aside.

In saucepan, melt butter over medium heat; whisk in brown sugar just until combined, being careful not to boil. Remove from heat; stir in almonds. Spread over crackers.

Bake in 375°F (190°C) oven until bubbly, about 10 minutes. Let cool on pan on rack for 10 minutes; cut into squares. *(Make-ahead: Store in airtight container for up to 3 days.)*

Makes 28 bars. PER BAR: about 137 cal, 1 g pro, 9 g total fat (4 g sat. fat), 14 g carb, 1 g fibre, 17 mg chol, 46 mg sodium, 45 mg potassium. % RDI: 2% calcium, 3% iron, 6% vit A, 2% folate.

best **TIPS** ever

- Serve the macaroons with strong coffee or tea to balance the sweetness of the cookies.
- Coconut comes in a variety of sweetnesses and textures. These macaroons have a bit airier texture thanks to the use of shredded – rather than flaked – coconut. The condensed milk and candied fruit add plenty of sweetness, so unsweetened coconut is the right choice.

Peanut Butter Caramel Sundae Sauce

Sticky, gooey and utterly scrumptious, this sauce is the ultimate partner for ice cream. Sprinkle your sundae with salted roasted peanuts for a taste explosion.

¼ cup **unsalted butter**

½ cup packed **brown sugar**

¼ cup **granulated sugar**

¼ cup **golden corn syrup**

¼ tsp **salt**

⅓ cup **whipping cream (35%)**

½ cup **smooth peanut butter**

In saucepan, melt butter over medium-low heat; stir in brown sugar, granulated sugar, corn syrup, 2 tbsp water and salt. Cook, stirring, until thickened, about 5 minutes.

Stir in cream; cook for 30 seconds. Remove from heat.

Stir in peanut butter; let cool. Serve warm or at room temperature. *(Make-ahead: Refrigerate in airtight container for up to 1 week.)*

Makes about 1⅔ cups. PER 2 TBSP: about 170 cal, 3 g pro, 10 g total fat (5 g sat. fat), 19 g carb, 1 g fibre, 17 mg chol, 101 mg sodium, 98 mg potassium. % RDI: 1% calcium, 2% iron, 5% vit A, 4% folate.

family favourite desserts

Vanilla Pudding This sweet and simple pudding is much fresher and tastier than store-bought.

½ cup **granulated sugar**

3 tbsp **cornstarch**

2¼ cups **milk**

2 **eggs**

2 tsp **vanilla**

In saucepan, whisk sugar with cornstarch; whisk in milk. Stir over medium heat just until steaming.

In large bowl, whisk eggs; whisk in half of the hot milk mixture in slow steady stream. Gradually whisk back into pan; cook over medium-low heat, whisking, until thickened, about 15 minutes. Stir in vanilla.

Transfer to bowl; place plastic wrap directly on surface. Refrigerate until chilled, about 2 hours. *(Make-ahead: Refrigerate for up to 2 days.)*

Makes 6 servings. PER SERVING: about 150 cal, 5 g pro, 4 g total fat (1 g sat. fat), 25 g carb, 0 g fibre, 68 mg chol, 64 mg sodium, 147 mg potassium. % RDI: 11% calcium, 2% iron, 9% vit A, 6% folate.

Rich Fudgy Brownies These brownies are best made a day ahead – they get even fudgier!

6 oz (175 g) **semisweet chocolate,** chopped

¾ cup **granulated sugar**

¾ cup **butter,** cut in pieces

1 tsp **vanilla**

2 **eggs**

1 cup **all-purpose flour**

½ cup chopped **walnuts,** toasted

In saucepan, melt together chocolate, sugar and butter. Remove from heat and stir in vanilla; let cool for 10 minutes.

Whisk in eggs, 1 at a time; whisk in flour and walnuts. Scrape into greased foil-lined 8-inch (2 L) square cake pan.

Bake in 350°F (180°C) oven until cake tester inserted in centre comes out with a few moist crumbs clinging, 30 to 35 minutes. Let cool in pan on rack. Cut into squares. *(Make-ahead: Store in airtight container for up to 2 days.)*

Makes 16 pieces. PER PIECE: about 226 cal, 3 g pro, 15 g total fat (8 g sat. fat), 23 g carb, 1 g fibre, 50 mg chol, 98 mg sodium. % RDI: 1% calcium, 6% iron, 9% vit A, 6% folate.

Old-Fashioned Blueberry Pie

Berry pies like this one are worth the work – especially when tiny, sweet wild blueberries are in season. Top each slice with whipped cream or a dollop of creamy, tangy crème fraîche.

5 cups **fresh blueberries**

¾ cup **granulated sugar**

¼ cup **all-purpose flour**

½ tsp grated **lemon zest**

1 tbsp **lemon juice**

½ tsp **cinnamon**

1 **egg yolk**

PASTRY:

2½ cups **all-purpose flour**

½ tsp **salt**

½ cup cold **butter,** cubed (see Tip, below)

½ cup cold **lard,** cubed

¼ cup **ice water** (approx)

3 tbsp **sour cream**

PASTRY: In bowl, whisk flour with salt. Using pastry blender or 2 knives, cut in butter and lard until mixture is in fine crumbs with a few larger pieces. Whisk ice water with sour cream; drizzle over dry ingredients, stirring briskly with fork to form ragged dough and adding more water, 1 tbsp at a time, if too dry. Divide in half; press into discs. Wrap each in plastic wrap; refrigerate until chilled, about 30 minutes.

In large bowl, combine blueberries, sugar, flour, lemon zest, lemon juice and cinnamon; set aside.

On lightly floured surface, roll out half of the pastry to generous ⅛-inch (3 mm) thickness; fit into 9-inch (23 cm) pie plate. Trim to leave ¾-inch (2 cm) overhang. Scrape in filling.

Roll out remaining pastry. Whisk egg yolk with 1 tbsp water; brush over pastry rim. Arrange pastry over filling; trim to leave ¾-inch (2 cm) overhang. Fold overhang under bottom pastry rim; seal and flute edge.

Bake on bottom rack in 425°F (220°C) oven for 15 minutes. Reduce heat to 350°F (180°C); bake until golden and filling is thickened, 35 to 45 minutes. Let cool on rack.

Makes 8 to 10 servings. PER EACH OF 10 SERVINGS: about 382 cal, 4 g pro, 19 g total fat (10 g sat. fat), 49 g carb, 3 g fibre, 53 mg chol, 169 mg sodium. % RDI: 2% calcium, 12% iron, 9% vit A, 12% vit C, 32% folate.

best
TIPS
ever

Cold butter and/or lard ensures a flaky crust. When cubing or cutting in, touch them as little as possible – your body heat can melt the fat, which won't allow the pastry to develop all those tasty layers.

Ricotta Cheesecake With Citrus Compote

A perfect ending to a meal, this cheesecake is lighter than a traditional one made with only cream cheese. The small amounts of light cream cheese and light sour cream added to the ricotta make it creamy.

1 cup **graham wafer crumbs**

2 tbsp **butter,** melted

FILLING:

12 oz (340 g) **ricotta cheese**

8 oz (225 g) **light cream cheese,** softened

½ cup **granulated sugar**

2 **eggs**

½ cup **light sour cream**

2 tbsp **all-purpose flour**

2 tsp **vanilla**

1½ tsp grated **orange zest**

CITRUS COMPOTE:

2 **oranges**

2 **pink grapefruit**

½ tsp **cornstarch**

Stir crumbs with butter until moistened; press into bottom of greased 8-inch (2 L) springform pan. Place on large square of foil; press foil up around side of pan. Bake in 350°F (180°C) oven until crust is firm, about 8 minutes. Let cool.

FILLING: In food processor, purée together ricotta cheese, cream cheese and sugar until smooth. Blend in eggs, 1 at a time. Blend in sour cream, flour, vanilla and orange zest. Pour over baked crust.

Set foil-wrapped pan in larger pan; pour in enough hot water to come 1 inch (2.5 cm) up side. Bake in 325°F (160°C) oven until set, 50 to 60 minutes. Remove from water. Run knife around edge of cake; remove foil and let cool on rack. Cover and refrigerate for 8 hours. *(Make-ahead: Refrigerate for up to 2 days.)*

CITRUS COMPOTE: Cut peel and white pith off oranges and grapefruit; working over bowl to catch juice, cut between membranes and fruit to release segments. Let stand for 10 minutes. Drain juice into small saucepan; stir in cornstarch. Bring to boil over medium heat; cook until thickened, about 3 minutes. Stir back into fruit mixture; let cool to room temperature. Serve with cheesecake.

Makes 8 servings. PER SERVING: about 342 cal, 12 g pro, 17 g total fat (10 g sat. fat), 37 g carb, 2 g fibre, 97 mg chol, 290 mg sodium, 327 mg potassium. % RDI: 17% calcium, 7% iron, 25% vit A, 58% vit C, 14% folate.

more lightened-up desserts

Chocolate Banana Pudding
This cooked custard pudding, thickened with egg whites and cornstarch, has a creamy consistency without a lot of added fat. For old-fashioned chocolate pudding, simply omit the banana.

2¼ cups **milk**

⅔ cup **granulated sugar**

2 **egg whites**

⅓ cup **cocoa powder,** sifted

3 tbsp **cornstarch**

2 tsp **vanilla**

1 **banana**

In heavy-bottomed saucepan, combine 2 cups of the milk with sugar; cook, stirring often, just until bubbles form around edge of pan, about 5 minutes.

Meanwhile, in bowl, whisk together remaining milk, egg whites, cocoa powder and cornstarch; gradually whisk in hot milk mixture. Pour into clean saucepan; cook over medium heat, stirring, until consistency of melted chocolate, about 10 minutes. Let cool slightly; stir in vanilla.

Pour into clean bowl; place plastic wrap directly on surface. Refrigerate until chilled, about 2 hours. *(Make-ahead: Refrigerate for up to 2 days.)*

Just before serving, dice banana; stir into pudding.

Makes 4 servings. PER SERVING: about 285 cal, 8 g pro, 5 g total fat (3 g sat. fat), 56 g carb, 3 g fibre, 10 mg chol, 152 mg sodium. % RDI: 16% calcium, 7% iron, 7% vit A, 3% vit C, 4% folate.

Apple Cherry Strudel Roll

This combo of phyllo, apples and cherries is a luscious, flaky alternative to regular apple pie. Serve with whipped cream, vanilla ice cream or frozen yogurt if you want a little extra indulgence.

8 sheets **phyllo pastry**

¼ cup **unsalted butter,** melted

2 tsp **icing sugar**

Pinch **cinnamon**

FILLING:

4 **tart apples** (such as Braeburn), peeled and finely chopped

⅔ cup **dried cherries** (see Tips, below)

¼ cup packed **brown sugar**

3 tbsp **all-purpose flour**

¾ tsp **cinnamon**

Place 9-inch (2.5 L) springform pan on large square of foil; press foil up around side of pan. Set aside.

FILLING: Toss together apples, cherries, brown sugar, flour and cinnamon; set aside.

Place 1 phyllo sheet on work surface, keeping remainder covered with damp tea towel to prevent drying out. Brush lightly with butter. Top with second sheet; brush lightly with butter.

Leaving ½-inch (1 cm) border at each end, spread one-quarter of the filling in strip along 1 long edge of phyllo. Fold ends over and roll up firmly; brush lightly with butter. Place roll, seam side down, around edge of prepared pan. Repeat to make 3 more rolls, fitting each into pan to make spiral and cover bottom.

Bake on bottom rack in 425°F (220°C) oven for 15 minutes. Reduce heat to 375°F (190°C) and bake until golden and crisp, about 50 minutes.

Remove foil; let cool in pan on rack for 15 minutes. Run knife around edge of pan. Remove side of pan; transfer to cake plate (see Tips, below). *(Make-ahead: Set aside at room temperature for up to 4 hours. Reheat in 375°F/190°C oven for about 20 minutes.)*

Sprinkle with icing sugar and cinnamon. Serve warm.

Makes 6 servings. PER SERVING: about 324 cal, 4 g pro, 9 g total fat (5 g sat. fat), 60 g carb, 4 g fibre, 21 mg chol, 201 mg sodium. % RDI: 2% calcium, 7% iron, 8% vit A, 10% vit C.

best **TIPS** ever

- Use tart dried cherries in this strudel for best flavour. Or try dried cranberries or raisins.

- To transfer the strudel from the pan to a serving plate neatly, slide a palette knife or a long, wide lifter underneath it.

Classic Tarte Tatin
A gorgeous skillet pie like this deserves a place of pride on the table. It's always nice with whipped cream, but it might be even better with a good old-fashioned slice of sharp Cheddar cheese.

1 cup **all-purpose flour**

1 tbsp **granulated sugar**

Pinch **salt**

½ cup cold **butter,** quartered

1 **egg yolk**

2 tbsp **ice water**

FILLING:

3¼ lb (1.4 kg) **Crispin apples**
   (8 to 10 apples)

⅓ cup **butter,** softened

1 cup **granulated sugar**

In bowl, stir flour, sugar and salt. With pastry blender, cut in butter until in coarse crumbs. Whisk egg yolk with ice water; drizzle over flour mixture and toss with fork until in clumps. With floured hands, form into ball; press into 1-inch (2.5 cm) thick disc. Wrap and refrigerate for 30 minutes.

FILLING: Meanwhile, peel, quarter and core apples; set aside. Spread butter over 8- or 9-inch (20 or 23 cm) cast-iron skillet that is at least 2½ inches (6 cm) deep. Sprinkle evenly with sugar. Set apple wedges upright in sugar, wedging tightly to fill skillet. Cook over medium heat, uncovered and basting occasionally, until syrup is thickened and apples are light caramel brown, 30 to 40 minutes.

Test apples with fork; if tips are not tender, bake skillet in 375°F (190°C) oven until tender, about 10 minutes. Let cool in refrigerator until no longer steaming, about 10 minutes.

On lightly floured surface, roll out pastry into circle slightly larger than top of skillet. Trim edge if necessary. Roll loosely around rolling pin; unroll over apples, tucking between pan and apples. Cut 4 steam vents in centre.

Bake in 425°F (220°C) oven for 10 minutes. Reduce heat to 375°F (190°C); bake until crust is golden, 15 to 20 minutes. Let cool for 3 to 4 minutes.

Invert heatproof platter over tarte. Wearing oven mitts, turn skillet upside down onto platter. With spatula, remove any apples stuck to skillet and arrange on tarte. Spoon syrup over top. Let cool slightly before cutting into wedges.

Makes 6 to 8 servings. PER EACH OF 8 SERVINGS: about 406 cal, 3 g pro, 20 g total fat (12 g sat. fat), 57 g carb, 2 g fibre, 76 mg chol, 137 mg sodium, 155 mg potassium. % RDI: 2% calcium, 6% iron, 18% vit A, 7% vit C, 16% folate.

classic french desserts

Chocolate Hazelnut Pots de Crème

Chocolate and hazelnut is one of those flavour pairings that just about everyone can agree on. Here, it's incorporated into silky, rich individual custards for an elegant make-ahead dessert.

6 oz (175 g) **bittersweet chocolate,** chopped

2 cups **whipping cream (35%)**

6 **egg yolks**

⅓ cup **granulated sugar**

2 tbsp **hazelnut liqueur** or almond liqueur

Dash **vanilla**

1 tbsp chopped **hazelnuts,** toasted

Place chocolate in heatproof bowl. In saucepan, bring 1½ cups of the cream just to boil; pour over chocolate and stir until melted.

In separate bowl, whisk egg yolks with sugar; whisk in one-third of the chocolate mixture. Stir in remaining chocolate mixture, hazelnut liqueur and vanilla. Pour into six 3½- x 1½-inch (175 mL) ramekins or custard cups; place in 13- x 9-inch (3.5 L) cake pan. Pour in enough boiling water to come halfway up sides of ramekins.

Bake in 325°F (160°C) oven until set around edge but still slightly jiggly in centre, about 20 minutes. Remove ramekins from pan; let cool on rack to room temperature. Cover and refrigerate until chilled. *(Make-ahead: Refrigerate for up to 24 hours.)*

Whip remaining cream. With piping bag or spoon, pipe or spoon onto centre of each serving. Garnish with hazelnuts.

Makes 6 servings. PER SERVING: about 536 cal, 8 g pro, 50 g total fat (28 g sat. fat), 25 g carb, 4 g fibre, 323 mg chol, 40 mg sodium. % RDI: 9% calcium, 18% iron, 36% vit A, 11% folate.

Raspberry Napoleons With Tangerine Sabayon

The supereasy raspberry sauce makes 1½ cups, which is more than you need for this recipe. But the leftovers are terrific drizzled over ice cream and other desserts.

Half pkg (397 g pkg) **puff pastry,** thawed (see Tip, below)

1½ cups **fresh raspberries**

1 tbsp **granulated sugar**

1 tbsp **framboise** or raspberry liqueur

Icing sugar

RASPBERRY SAUCE:

⅔ lb (300 g) **frozen unsweetened raspberries,** thawed

2 tbsp **granulated sugar**

1 tsp **lemon juice**

TANGERINE SABAYON:

3 **egg yolks**

3 tbsp **granulated sugar**

⅓ cup **tangerine juice**

2 tbsp **amber rum**

½ cup **whipping cream (35%)**

On floured surface, roll out pastry into 12-inch (30 cm) square. Cut crosswise into quarters; cut each into thirds to make 12 rectangles. Arrange on parchment paper–lined rimmed baking sheet; prick all over with fork. Refrigerate until chilled, about 2 hours. *(Make-ahead: Refrigerate for up to 24 hours.)*

Bake in 400°F (200°C) oven until slightly puffed and golden, 15 to 18 minutes. Set aside. *(Make-ahead: Store in airtight container for up to 8 hours.)*

RASPBERRY SAUCE: In blender or food processor, purée together raspberries, ¼ cup water, sugar and lemon juice until smooth; press through fine-mesh sieve to remove seeds. *(Make-ahead: Cover and refrigerate for up to 1 week.)*

TANGERINE SABAYON: In heatproof bowl, whisk egg yolks with sugar until slightly thickened and pale. Whisk in tangerine juice and rum. Place over saucepan of gently simmering water. Whisking constantly, cook until thickened and mixture mounds slightly when dropped from whisk, 5 minutes. Immediately place bowl in larger bowl filled with ice water; whisk until cold. Whip cream; fold into chilled sabayon. *(Make-ahead: Cover; refrigerate for up to 8 hours.)*

Mix raspberries, sugar and framboise. *(Make-ahead: Cover and refrigerate for up to 2 hours; bring to room temperature.)*

Drizzle 2 tbsp raspberry sauce onto each of 4 dessert plates; top each with 1 piece of the pastry. Top with 2 tbsp each of the sabayon and berry mixture. Top with second piece of the pastry; repeat sabayon and berry layers once. Top with remaining pastry; dust with icing sugar.

Makes 4 servings. PER SERVING: about 533 cal, 7 g pro, 34 g total fat (10 g sat. fat), 48 g carb, 4 g fibre, 182 mg chol, 141 mg sodium, 190 mg potassium. % RDI: 5% calcium, 16% iron, 19% vit A, 30% vit C, 25% folate.

best **TIPS** ever

You'll have a leftover square of puff pastry from these napoleons. Save it for making a quick batch of cheese straws or fruit turnovers. Or use it instead of pie pastry to top off little crocks of your favourite chicken pot pie filling.

Chocolate Layer Cake A favourite in The Test Kitchen, this cake is a classic that never goes out of style. It's perfectly chocolaty for any celebration.

1 cup **butter,** softened

1½ cups **granulated sugar**

2 **eggs**

1 tsp **vanilla**

2 cups **all-purpose flour**

½ cup **cocoa powder**

1 tsp each **baking powder** and **baking soda**

¼ tsp **salt**

1½ cups **buttermilk**

CHOCOLATE ICING:

1½ cups **butter,** softened

½ cup **whipping cream (35%)**

1 tbsp **vanilla**

3 cups **icing sugar**

6 oz (175 g) **unsweetened chocolate,** chopped, melted and cooled

In large bowl, beat butter with sugar until fluffy. Beat in eggs, 1 at a time; beat in vanilla. Sift together flour, cocoa powder, baking powder, baking soda and salt. Stir into butter mixture alternately with buttermilk, making 3 additions of dry ingredients and 2 of buttermilk.

Spoon into 2 greased then parchment paper–lined 9-inch (1.5 L) round cake pans; smooth tops. Bake in 350°F (180°C) oven until cake tester inserted in centre comes out clean, 30 to 35 minutes. Let cool in pans on racks for 20 minutes. Invert onto racks; peel off paper. Let cool completely. *(Make-ahead: Wrap separately in plastic wrap and refrigerate for up to 24 hours. Or overwrap in heavy-duty foil and freeze for up to 2 weeks.)* Cut each cake horizontally into 2 layers.

CHOCOLATE ICING: In bowl, beat butter until fluffy; gradually beat in cream. Beat in vanilla. Beat in icing sugar, about 1 cup at a time. Beat in chocolate until fluffy.

Place 1 layer, cut side up, on cake plate. Slide strips of waxed paper between cake and plate. Spread cut side with about ¾ cup of the icing; cover with another layer, cut side down. Spread top with another ¾ cup of the icing. Repeat with remaining layers. Spread remaining icing over side and top. Remove paper strips. *(Make-ahead: Cover loosely; refrigerate for up to 2 days. Bring to room temperature before serving.)*

Makes 16 to 20 servings. PER EACH OF 20 SERVINGS: about 464 cal, 4 g pro, 31 g total fat (19 g sat. fat), 47 g carb, 2 g fibre, 89 mg chol, 296 mg sodium. % RDI: 5% calcium, 11% iron, 23% vit A, 14% folate.

change it up

Chocolate Cupcakes: Spoon batter into 24 greased or paper-lined muffin cups. Decrease baking time to 20 minutes. Transfer to racks; let cool. Spread tops with icing.

Makes 24 cupcakes.

best easy cakes

Mango Swirl Ice-Cream Cake
This refreshing dessert is ideal for any occasion, but it's especially nice after a spicy meal. Vary the flavour of the sorbet and the fruit, and you can reinvent this cake time and time again.

4 cups **mango sorbet,** softened

4 cups **vanilla ice cream,** softened

3 cups **assorted fresh fruit** (such as blueberries, raspberries, sliced strawberries and sliced peeled peaches)

CRUST:

1¼ cups **graham wafer crumbs**

¼ cup finely chopped **pecans**

¼ cup **butter,** melted

Grease bottom of 9-inch (2.5 L) springform pan; line side with parchment paper. Set aside.

CRUST: In bowl, stir together crumbs, pecans and butter until moistened; press into prepared pan. Bake in 350°F (180°C) oven until firm, about 10 minutes. Let cool in pan on rack.

Drop spoonfuls of half of the sorbet randomly onto crust. Drop spoonfuls of half of the ice cream in gaps between sorbet. Gently swirl with back of spoon, filling all gaps. Repeat with remaining sorbet and ice cream. Cover and freeze until firm, about 4 hours. *(Make-ahead: Wrap in foil and freeze for up to 2 days.)*

Using hot dry knife (see Tip, below), cut cake into slices. Serve with fruit.

Makes 8 to 10 servings. PER EACH OF 10 SERVINGS: about 335 cal, 4 g pro, 14 g total fat (7 g sat. fat), 52 g carb, 2 g fibre, 35 mg chol, 159 mg sodium. % RDI: 8% calcium, 6% iron, 17% vit A, 27% vit C, 8% folate.

change it up
Mini Mango Swirl Ice-Cream Cake: Use 6-inch (1 L) springform pan. Reduce ice cream to 1 cup. Reduce remaining ingredients by half.

Makes 6 servings.

best **TIPS** ever

A hot dry knife makes neat, clean slices of this frozen cake. Run the knife under hot water and dry it well with a towel before slicing.

Carrot Snacking Cake

This all-purpose cake is simple, delicious and wholesome. It's also a lot easier to make than a traditional carrot cake with cream cheese icing. You can substitute a dusting of icing sugar for the glaze if you prefer.

¾ cup **canned crushed pineapple**

2 **eggs**

¾ cup **granulated sugar**

⅓ cup **vegetable oil**

¼ cup **unsweetened applesauce**

1 tsp **vanilla**

1¼ cups **all-purpose flour**

1 tsp **cinnamon**

1 tsp **baking powder**

½ tsp **baking soda**

¼ tsp **salt**

1½ cups grated **carrots**

½ cup **golden raisins** (optional)

PINEAPPLE GLAZE:

1 cup **icing sugar**

In fine-mesh sieve set over bowl, drain pineapple, pressing to extract juice. Set juice and pineapple aside separately.

In large bowl, beat eggs with sugar until pale. Beat in oil, applesauce and vanilla. Whisk together flour, cinnamon, baking powder, baking soda and salt; stir into egg mixture just until moistened. Stir in pineapple, carrots, and raisins (if using). Scrape into parchment paper–lined 9-inch (2.5 L) square cake pan.

Bake in 350°F (180°C) oven until cake tester inserted in centre comes out clean, about 45 minutes. Let cool in pan on rack for 15 minutes. Remove from pan; let cool completely. *(Make-ahead: Wrap and store for up to 2 days or overwrap in foil and freeze in airtight container for up to 2 weeks.)*

PINEAPPLE GLAZE: Whisk icing sugar with 2 tbsp of the reserved pineapple juice, adding up to 1 tsp more juice, if necessary, to make spreadable. Spread over cake. Let stand until set, about 1 hour.

Makes 16 pieces. PER PIECE: about 162 cal, 2 g pro, 5 g total fat (1 g sat. fat), 27 g carb, 1 g fibre, 23 mg chol, 108 mg sodium. % RDI: 2% calcium, 5% iron, 17% vit A, 3% vit C, 11% folate.

index

acknowledgments

This second volume of *Best Recipes Ever* is the product of many imaginations and so much hard work.

It takes many talented people to produce Canada's most-watched daily food show, but the *Best Recipes Ever* team makes it look easy. CBC would like to thank the following people for their contributions to this delicious endeavour:

- Chef Christine Tizzard, who stepped in so effortlessly as the new host of the show, sharing her passion for making family-friendly food with Canadians across the nation every afternoon

- No great idea takes off without the support of the people in charge. Special thanks go to CBC executives Kirstine Stewart and Julie Bristow, as well as head of factual entertainment Jennifer Dettman, and production executive Grazyna Krupa for their continued belief in the series, and CBC Licencing's Karen Bower for making this book a reality

- Here's to Krista Look, executive producer/creator of *Best Recipes Ever*, and her fabulous behind-the-scenes production team: Portia Corman, Thérèse Attard, Jonah Snitman, Flo Leung, Josie Malevich, Andrée Soulière, and the producers, food folks, production assistants, directors, crew and editors who make it all happen

Cookbook production is also done by a huge cast of characters. *Canadian Living* would like to thank the following people for their work on this book:

- *Canadian Living* food director Annabelle Waugh and her team, The Canadian Living Test Kitchen, for their creative and tasty vision, which has brought these tried-and-tested recipes into existence

- Art directors Chris Bond and Colin Elliott for their mouthwatering art direction and design, and project editor Tina Anson Mine for dotting all the i's and crossing all the t's on this project

- Photographers Jodi Pudge and Edward Pond, food stylists Ashley Denton and Claire Stubbs, and prop stylist Catherine Doherty for creating the beautiful new images for this book. And thanks to many more photographers and stylists for the other gorgeous photos in these pages (see the back cover for a complete list)

- Copy editor Brenda Thompson for her eagle eye and dedication to making sure every line of every paragraph was just perfect, and Beth Zabloski, our indexer, for assembling an easy-to-navigate index

- Sharyn Joliat of Info Access for complete, accurate nutrient analysis, and Random House Canada for distribution and promotion of this book

- Transcontinental Books vice-president Marc Laberge, publishing director Mathieu De Lajartre and assistant editor Céline Comtois for the million details they manage throughout the entire publishing process

- *Canadian Living* publisher Caroline Andrews, executive director of brand development Susan Antonacci and editor-in-chief Jennifer Reynolds for championing *Canadian Living* books

150 ESSENTIAL **WHOLE GRAIN RECIPES**

The **AFFORDABLE FEASTS** *Collection*

THE
Barbecue
COLLECTION

The International Collection

THE One Dish COLLECTION

The Complete PRESERVING Book

ALSO AVAILABLE FROM
Transcontinental Books